EXCELLER
SELECT

TOP PICKS

Awaken

&

Heal

Awaken

&

Heal

Enlightenment for Your Soul

Sibonelo Mbhele

EXCELLER BOOKS™
A GLOBAL PRESS

Awaken & Heal
Enlightenment for Your Soul

Copyright © Sibonelo Mbhele, South Africa, 2024

Cover by Exceller Books using resources from Pixabay.com

All rights reserved. No portion of the book may or should be reproduced, stored in any retrieval system (including but not limited to computers, disks, external drives, electronic or digital devices, e-readers, websites), or transmitted in any form or by any means (mechanical, recording, electronic, digital version, photocopying, or otherwise) without the prior, written permission of the publisher, nor be otherwise circulated in any form of binding or cover other than that in which it is published and without a similar condition being imposed on the subsequent purchaser.

The book has been published with all reasonable efforts taken to make the material error-free after the consent of the author. The views and opinions expressed in this book are the author's own and the facts are as reported by him. Neither the publisher nor editor endorse or approve the content of this book or guaranty the reliability, accuracy or completeness of the content published herein and do not make and representations of warranties of any kind, express or implied, including but not limited to the implied warranties of merchantability, fitness for a particular purpose. The publisher or editor shall not be liable whatsoever for any errors, omissions, whether such errors or omissions result from negligence, accident or any other cause or claims for loss or damage of any kind, including without limitation damage arising out of use, or about reliability, accuracy, sufficiency of the information contained in this book.

ISBN: 978-81-19524-71-6

First published in India in 2024 by Exceller Books,
An imprint of GE Group
Address: G1, Dream Apartment, Degree College Road, Belgharia, Kolkata, 700056, India

www.excellerbooks.com

Foreword

It gives me such a pleasure to be offered an opportunity to write a foreword to Sibonelo Mbhele's book, AWAKEN AND HEAL. Reading the book was like reading the unfolding of my own life story over the past 61 years of living here on Earth. I was touched by the various aspects of my upbringing and attachments that are contained in the book. Sibonelo Mbhele is definitely a visionary, a scholar and a devout lover of God. He is one of the global messengers pioneering the awakening of humanity that is so desperately needed in our times.

The human experience is the most traumatic and depressing experience that any self-conscious creature can go through. We are human beings having human experiences that are sometimes very traumatic and painful. Some even commit suicide to avoid the pain that goes with the human experience. This is life, and it is very difficult. Sibonelo has already eloquently elucidated the ups and downs of being human on this planet. It all begins the moment we are separated from the umbilical cord that made us feel oneness with the mother who carried us for nine months. We did not know who was carrying us, but we did experience the joy, warmth and pleasure of being carried without us having anything to do with the carrying. Then came the moment of separation from the one who carried us for nine months, and all hell broke loose. This is the hell that is so insightfully explained in this book. Both the biblical Job and Siddhartha Gautama said the human experience consists of suffering.

To be human is to be like a fly in a window. You don't know whether you'll survive by getting inside or staying outside. We fear attachment, and we fear detachment. The abuse of drugs and alcohol is related to attachment issues. Some people would rather spend the weekend in a bar than face reality. We suffer because we fell in love, and we suffer because we don't want to be trapped in love again. We are born attached. This attachment solidifies as we learn about culture and religion. As we grow into adulthood, it becomes almost impossible to detach from the attachment of so many years. As Eckhart Tolle says, "If you live in one culture for the first 20 years, you become conditioned without knowing it".

In the process of conditioning, we develop beliefs, which are simply solidified thoughts. Again, Eckhart Tolle elaborates on beliefs that we imbibed unknowingly; "Beliefs are not just simply beliefs to those who hold them, they are the Absolute Truth".

So many hold strongly to their beliefs, never questioning those beliefs, not realizing they accepted those beliefs as a little child. A little child has determined their fate and destiny, even in adulthood. Philosopher Ken Wilber says some people hold beliefs and value structures that even some four-year-old-child no longer holds. Some people are like trees, they take forever to grow up. Some people are just a grown-up four-year old. Period. Just check their beliefs.

Philosopher Ken Wilber has helped me a lot in understanding human complexity:
"From an Integral point of view, simply "Waking Up" isn't enough. We are also being called to "Grow Up" (mature emotionally), "Clean Up" (engage in shadow work), and "Show Up" (embody our insight in our daily lives). In ten to twenty years, which is really an extremely short time, we will see a dramatic shift in the population that will

understand, care and have concern for all people, regardless of race, colour, sex, or creed. This is called world-centric."

Even Psychologists, as Sibonelo has elucidated, struggle with all types of attachments that human beings have to go through. Let us also remember that these types of attachments evolve with time, age, region, circumstances and a host of other probabilities that we don't even know of. New attachments are discovered daily by human sciences. The human psyche contains mysterious depths from which all the symbols by which we give meaning and worth to human existence have come. The mystery and depth of the human psyche is what Psychologists and Psychiatrists have been baffled with since modernity evolved into the radar of our current life. Life has a way of throwing curveballs at us, unleashing suffering that even defies Psychologists and Psychiatrists. Some people are too lazy to work, while others become attached to working very long hours—week after week—for reasons known only by their hearts. "The heart has reasons of its own that even reason can never understand", said the 17th-century Philosopher Blaise Pascal. Father Richard Rohr says the fall from grace is an act of God, and the rise from the fall is also the act of God. The Chinese Philosophy says all of life is Yin and Yang (contraction and expansion). We have to embrace this life in its fullness if we are going to be peaceful. Live with both attachment and detachment. Live in solitude and the company of people. Find the balance and what works for you. The Buddha says everything should be done in moderation. Be moderately attached and moderately detached. Embrace your humanity in its fullness. This is what modern awakening is all about.

Let's not use meditation to bypass our issues with the world, including family matters. Let us not use stillness and silence to avoid the traumas of life. Let us not get rid of the ego to avoid our unresolved humanness. We are human beings. Period. It is natural to be attached, then detached, then confused, and end up in your own solitude. You then find yourself attached to solitude and have a negative feel to the presence of crowds. Someone once said, 'I love people but hate the crowds'.

We have human experiences, and we must take these experiences as they come. Our divinity lies at the depth of our humanity. We can no longer run to the caves and mountains to avoid the challenges of being human. We can't repress the unforgivable; we have to face it and even admit that, at this moment, we can't just forgive. Maybe later in the future, we will have the grace to forgive. That is being downright human. We can only save our species by embracing our full humanity. This is an awakening from the patriarchal faux religion that has been given to us over the years. We need to develop a human spirituality that is grounded in our humanness, our bodies, our feelings, our emotions and even our relationships with each other. It takes authenticity, vulnerability and honesty to be a real human. Not forced attachments or detachments. Not forced social availability or solitude.

Everyone has to be authentic and honest with themselves and others. I close with these wise words from Philosopher Ken Wilber: "I have one major rule: Everybody is right. More specifically, everybody—including me—has some important pieces of truth, and all of those pieces need to be honoured, cherished, and included in a more gracious, spacious, and compassionate embrace".

Let me end this foreword without taking away the essence of this beautifully written piece. Read this book with all of your beings. Don't read to finish it, but read it to contemplate the meaning of each sentence as it relates to your current life.

Muzwandile C. Cindi
Businessman & Author
Thailand, Asia.

Table of Contents

1| The Attachment — 11

2| The Power of Attachments — 20

3| The Inevitability of the Attachment — 31

4| The Attachment Paradox — 35

5| The Poignancy of Separation and Parting — 41

6| Memento Homo (Remember, You Are Only Human) — 50

7| Association and Isolation — 63

8| Need for Belonging and Acceptance — 67

9| Beyond the Separation Illusion — 71

10| False Hope Hurts — 86

11| Everything Is Burning — 96

12| Heal It or Relive It — 102

13| Finding Closure Heals Us — 110

14| Empty Yourself and Free Yourself — 119

15| Apology from Life to Humanity — 127

16| Prayer for Emotional Healing — 133

17| Prayer for Deep-Seated Traumas — 136

18| The Serenity Prayer — 138

Conclusion — 140

1 | The Attachment

Aimie Apigian, who is the leading medical expert on how life experiences get stored in the body, tells us that attachment is the development of a healthy nervous system. We initially think of the bond, the connection, and the relationship, but we don't often think that attachment is actually our nervous system. It is how it is wired. It is how it operates. Attachment is how our nervous system adapts best to survive our early childhood. Attachment is the degree of safety and security wired into our nervous system. Attachment is our pattern of insecurity or security with ourselves, others, and the world. Attachment is the internal degree of regulation that one has in their nervous system in relationship with the world, others and themselves.

She further tells us that our attachment is a result of repeated experiences that our nervous system adapted to and formed a strong memory with the help of neurochemicals and hormones. Our attachment patterns are our survival patterns. Our coping mechanisms, habits, relationships, mental health, energy level and physical health- all are our survival patterns locked into our nervous system. Attachment is a survival thing. The process of attachment starts even while we are in the womb. Attachment is formed much earlier than we used to think.

Attachment was thought to solidify by the age of one to three years. This is because it was measured through behaviour. Most of society is affected by attachment disruption. This process starts even while we are in the womb.

Moreover, Dr. Aimie states that attachment and bonding process starts before a baby is born. In the utero, the baby is physically attached to the mother. It requires physical attachment for survival. At birth, the baby undergoes a transition. In the womb, it was physically attached to the mother for survival. After birth, it moves to external physical attachment—not through the umbilical cord, but through the mother's touch and physical contact, which remain important.

Attachment is seeing the world as a generally safe place or generally unsafe place, depending on whether you have a secure or insecure attachment style. For those with an insecure attachment and the struggles it comes with, life becomes very difficult. It often becomes one's biggest pain in life and something they never rise above or change. When you come out of childhood with an insecure attachment, it is highly likely that you will experience trauma in future. Laurell K. Hamilton speaks of wounds that never show on the body, wounds that are deeper and more hurtful than anything that bleeds. I believe attachment is very much implicated in us human beings sustaining such wounds. We bear many wounds that do not show on our bodies, yet they are more hurtful than physical wounds.

Attachment is a visitor that comes unannounced, a guest that needs no invitation; you hear it approaching, but you never know when it will arrive. It knocks, and while you are still thinking of opening, you find that it has already entered. In the beginning, it shows us its light, and only later on does it reveal its shadows. If you are somebody who works with people, you most probably bear testimony to the fact that, without noticing it, you find yourself attached to those you are helping, sometimes developing possessiveness, which makes you feel as if you own them. Attachment is implicated in the development of possessiveness and feeling that we own people, especially those we have helped in some way, and this, in turn, hurts you, the helper. Attachment works with the ego only to hurt us in the end.

People are not bound to meet your expectations simply because you have helped them. Do not attach a sense of ownership to those you have helped, because you can never be sure how they will be once they are well. Sometimes, they may forget you not because they are evil but because they are human, and human beings do forget. Life has a way of getting in the way in a way that none of us can ever be fully prepared for.

Once attachment develops and is embraced by an individual, the strongest of assegais, the sharpest of daggers and the double edge of swords will have a tough time cutting it. It is a bond that leaves one bleeding when broken. It leaves the heart with emotional scars and the mind with psychological sores. Attachment is like an ancient pandemic without a cure. It preys on people's emotions; to cure individuals of it, they would have to be completely stripped of their emotions, which is nearly impossible. How we are conditioned from childhood is at the centre of most of our suffering.

A part of me agrees very much with David Benatar when he says coming into existence is harmful because had one not existed, one would have been spared of the many sufferings that are a part of being alive. But now that you have come into existence, it is your duty to handle the bitter and sweet of existence. After the command to be fruitful, multiply and fill the earth, we should have been told to brace ourselves for the unavoidable and painful costs of existence.

Attachment lies dormant inside people until its rightful subject comes to wake them from their sleep. Its development is a result of the interaction between the senses and the external world. It has often caused even the emotionally withdrawn and resistant to succumb to it. Out of many, only a few can resist it. Just as we choose our death by how we live, we also choose our pain and pleasure when we embrace and entertain a developing attachment. Attachment is like a dancing assassin.

You will bleed unexpectedly. You will move with the flow, and while you are dancing to its tune, the pain will come silently in an unsuspicious manner that will leave you devastated. Such is the case in relationships where disappointments and breakups occur when one least expects them to, and people are left with the heavy-duty of detaching and healing themselves.

I have seen parents finding it difficult to part with their children when time and age necessitate the parting; I have seen tears between lovers when breakups happen and discomfort when people must change their environment because of attachment. It develops between parents and children only to leave parents prone to what is called an 'empty nest syndrome,' feelings of sadness and loss when the last child leaves home. It is the mother of all ties, networks, and associations between human beings and human beings, human beings and objects and even human beings and their environments. It is not only limited to human beings but animals, too. I have often noticed how animal offspring, together with their parents, wail and groan when they are separated.

Separation is attachment's greatest opponent because, whereas separation opens a gap between two things or individuals, attachment thrives on oneness, closeness, and unity. Being too attached is often fearful because it deeply roots and greatly binds one to another or one to something to a point where one lives fully in the moment and completely forgets about the uncertainty of life. I remember a certain pastor who once expressed how he feared the way he was becoming attached to a little girl who was not biologically his and that he was raised together with his wife. His concern was that he loved that child so much, yet at the same time, the thought that one day the child might be taken away from them after they had become so close silently and secretly haunted him.

Attachment comes in different forms to different individuals, as psychologists claim that there are different styles of attachment; some individuals exhibit a secure form of attachment, welcoming contact and affection, and bonding with their significant other. Others display the resistant type of attachment; their bond with others is characterized by feelings of insecurity, and they tend to resist closeness with the object of their attachment, particularly after separation. At the same time, others have the avoidant type of attachment characterized by little separation protest and a tendency to avoid or ignore the significant other. Then there is the ambivalent-avoidant type that is highly characterized by the ambivalence or indifference of simultaneously wanting and avoiding attachment. You desire it but at the same time are afraid of it; the guy who stars in *Fifty Shades of Grey* displays this form of attachment when he wants to be needed by the woman, yet he intentionally chooses to be sexually available and emotionally unavailable.

Relationships, to a certain extent, are negatively affected by the fear of attachment, and the ego does not create nor allow for a safe outlet for this deep-seated fear. Personally, I am of the view that attachment is neither fixed nor stable; it can take different forms in one person and the same person in response to the external world. A person with a secure form of attachment can be altered by hurt or disappointment to exhibit the ambivalent avoidant type of attachment. None of us is without attachment; we just differ in how we manifest it.

Attachment is a universal language spoken by all of humanity differently, an experience wherein mankind has little choice because we are all born with an innate ability to attach. According to the basic doctrines of early Buddhism, existence is suffering, and suffering has a cause, namely craving and attachment. Even the enlightened of ancient times did see the implication of attachment in human suffering. Even arguments and conflicts erupt because of our attachment to our opinions and worldviews. When people are too attached to their opinions and convictions, it is highly likely that they will aggressively defend themselves and violently attack any difference of opinion without giving it fair consideration. An individual may be too attached to the need for social status to the point that they do not care who gets hurt for them to acquire and maintain it.

Controlling an attachment to something is always an individual's responsibility, and it begins with being aware of the attachment. Be aware of how much you are attached to your convictions. Be aware of how much you are attached to your opinions. Be aware of how much you are attached to the other. Be aware of your attachment to certain things. You cannot monitor and control what you are not aware of. Attachment is the cause of many people's pain. It hurts when you break up with your lover; it wounds you when you divorce your spouse; it tortures you when you lose your most valued possessions and it grieves you when your loved one passes away.

The pain is never directly caused by loss or separation but by the bond that was formed with what one is separated from. Raise your awareness of your attachments and increase your control of them. Most human experiences are self-generated. Even the pain of detachment is a result of many things that the mind has formed around what the person was attached to. From analysing attachment, it appears that who wounded me is me, and who wounded you is you. If human beings can bring themselves to the point of crying without a real cause in telenovelas, movies and dramas, that should give us a hint of our capability to generate our own experiences. Anything can easily irritate and provoke you if you are already angry on the inside, and anything can easily make you happy if you are already happy on the inside. In most cases, the external factors do not bring new emotions. Rather, they magnify and expose your emotional state. It is easy for someone who had a long day at work to be irritated and annoyed just by anything at home, and the opposite is true.

Attachment is the implicit cause of many explicit wounds. It externalizes itself so that people always have something to point at outside of themselves for their hurt and pain when the actual cause is right within them. When we increase our level of self-awareness, we gain control over ourselves, and we are, to a certain degree, able to heal ourselves. Dealing with the wound is only effective when you are aware of the actual cause. Attachment is a hidden torturer that appears in disguises so as not to be seen. The actual cause of the pain that comes with losing is not the loss itself but how attached, you were to what you lost. I am persuaded to believe that if we were attached to nothing, we would be hurt by nothing. It is our responsibility to know when attachment is serving us and when it is hurting us because treasuring it, even when it hurts us, comes with a high price of losing ourselves.

"Nonresistance, nonjudgement, and nonattachment are the three aspects of true freedom and enlightened living."

– Eckhart Tolle

2 | The Power of Attachments

Its grip is as strong as the pain it leaves. It can develop easily, but it will deteriorate with difficulty. Wide is its entrance, but narrow is the exit. It possesses and controls those who embrace and entertain it. You may think you are in control of it, but as time goes by, you will realize that you are under its power. Things that used to be a choice now become a must. You can no longer sleep without calling that special someone. You no longer feel complete if a day passes by without seeing them, and they no longer cross your mind but permanently dwell in it.

An attachment is an addiction without any formal rehabilitation; it takes longer to detach than to attach. Once it gets a hold of you, you will escape with difficulty. It has the power to unveil the hidden weakness and fragility even in the strongest individuals. It has its own way of pervading even the most fortified chambers of an individual's heart. It turns hearts into leaders and minds into servants, and when that happens, tragedy is bound to abound. Mothers can even attach to their unborn babies and grieve greatly if the delivery of the conceived fetus happens to be unsuccessful; that is just how powerful attachment is.

One cannot fully barricade nor sufficiently armour oneself for the fight against this force. There are no physical weapons for defence; it is a battle of the mind and heart. You have no fear of attachment if you have never been hurt by it. I have often noticed how attached individuals can be, especially females, to their partners when they are in a romantic relationship for the first time. It is only after an individual has been hurt or disappointed by his or her object of attachment that they no longer give in fully to attachment. The pain of attachment always outlasts its pleasure. The power of attachment may be great in the beginning but degenerates with time.

Like its pain that is healed over time, its power is also weakened at the very same time. When two things are tightly bonded, they need a force of some sort to be separated. Depending on how strong the bond is, the force that separates two joined things might need to be applied over time for it to be able to accomplish the separation. It is common to hear couples who have been through a lot eventually saying they are tired of fighting. This means it took time for the forces that were fighting their bond to finally break their bond; they had been through a lot of challenges but resisted, but just because they were resisting, it did not necessarily mean the challenges were without any effect on their relationship.

To fully yield to an attachment is to fully yield to its pain. An attachment is a bond that subjects one to bondage; you cannot claim to be free when you are attached. You lose your freedom the day you give your heart to someone or something. It becomes so much a part of you that it controls you and determines your priorities. As a twin, I am more concerned about what happens to my twin brother, family and loved ones than I am about myself. We unconsciously lose ourselves through attachment. Our hearts and lives stop being ours the day we become attached to certain individuals or things.

I once had a neighbour who had just bought a new car; in the morning, he would tell me that he woke up during the night just to check if it was still there and to ensure that the gate was locked. We sacrifice our joy, compromise our happiness, and even give up our own lives to see the other happy. Those you are attached to are your weakness, as they are your strength. If you want to start a fight with someone, touch those they are attached to and watch how they react. You live for that which you are attached to, and anything you live for, you can most certainly die for.

In the book of Genesis, after a woman was created, when man saw her, he said, "She is the bone of my bone and flesh of my flesh". The Bible goes further to say the two shall become one. The bone is the strongest part of our structure, while the flesh is the softest. When you are one with someone, you are one with their weaknesses and strengths. It comes naturally to act for the preservation, well-being, and welfare of those you are attached to. We are attached to that which we love. You cannot attach without love; you must first love something to be attached to it.

Attachment can almost be with anything; it does not necessarily have to be with a living thing. One can be in pain from losing something, such as a cellphone or any gadget they have owned for a long time. Even when they are not carrying it, they feel incomplete. As I said in my opening statement, to fully yield to an attachment is to fully yield to its pain. Parting with what you have been attached to for a long time is as painful as the removal of skin from the flesh; it leaves nothing but blood. It can cause even the most rational individual to act irrationally; as the saying goes, 'If you have never acted foolish for love, you've never loved at all'.

There are many who are bleeding inwardly because of former attachments; some have even gone to the extent of taking their own lives because of it. In a movie I once watched, there was a man who was a very powerful warrior. Being the main character in the story, he fought and killed a very strong and powerful antagonist who had terrorized, intimidated, and killed many. So, as he fought the antagonist, his wife was buried alive by this very antagonist in a coffin. The battle continued between the protagonist and the antagonist until the antagonist was defeated. Sadly, the main character's wife, who had been buried alive by this antagonist, suffocated until she died. When the main character finally came to rescue her, she was dead, and because he loved her so much, he could not bear her death and turned into a drunkard. When those who knew him from the war asked where the mighty warrior they knew had gone, he would reply, *"He died with his wife"*.

After having fought and defeated the strongest of opponents, he himself was overpowered by attachment. As

I carefully paid attention to his ending, I then learnt something very profound, 'love is good, but an excessive attachment can be fatal when it reaches a point where it does not let go even when time and circumstance necessitate'. If you say something or someone is your life, be careful because they can most likely be your death, too.

There is a part of us that dies with those we are attached to if the attachment is excessive. A person can be killed and buried by both the power and the pain of attachment. Power and pain are the two most dangerous 'Ps' of the attachment. Its power will lay hold of you while its pain tears you apart. If you yield to its power, you will enjoy its pleasure but also brace yourself to endure its pain. Our greatest pain is wrapped in our greatest joy, and sorrow is revealed when disappointment removes the wrap. It is common to see people shedding tears during moments of joy because our joyful moments have their own way of reminding us of the sorrows we have been through. That which excites you the most is also that which can hurt you the most. Pleasure is very dangerous; even the things that are destructive to you as an individual can give you pleasure. People find pleasure in drugs, sex, alcohol and so forth. It is rare to think of the repercussions of one's actions during pleasurable moments; it is only when the moment of pleasure ceases that reality strikes.

Pain and pleasure are never far from each other, no matter how distant they may seem at any given moment. There was a day when I was very happy, and a certain guy said to me, "Do not be too happy, brother. Something painful might happen". Back then, I never paid much attention to his statements, but now, it is coming back to me as a confirmation that some people are indeed aware of how intertwined and inseparable pleasure is from pain. Others, like King Solomon in the Bible, went to the extent of preferring pain over pleasure. In his exact words, he puts it as *"Better to be in a house of mourning than in the house of feasting"*. Pleasure is transient; it vanishes while you are still lost in it. Hence, Solomon cannot be blamed for his preference for mourning over feasting. You may be happy that you have conquered a certain battle today, only to find yourself fighting another tomorrow. Suffering and pain are denser and more solid than laughter and pleasure. When we make peace with how life works, we find peace within ourselves.

There is no warrior when it comes to attachment; we are all made vulnerable by our attachments. In one of Siddhartha Gautama's teachings, he said, *"Do not trust too much. Do not love too much. Do not hope too much because that too much can hurt you so much"*. If you are to love wastefully, it should be yourself. If you are to trust wholeheartedly, it should be God. The Bible teaches us that our first love should be our Creator, *"love the Lord your God with all your heart, mind, soul and your strength and secondly, you should love your neighbour as yourself"*.

This commandment is sequential; it is love for God first and love of self-second, which is then transferred to the neighbour; if there is no love of self, there cannot be love for neighbour. To minimize pain, adhere to this sequence the way it is; if you twist it, you only maximize your chances of pain and misery. The first love is directed to God, and it is specific in terms of how it should be; it should be love with your entire being. As for the love of self and neighbour, it is not specified, but the same magnitude of love towards the self should be the same towards the other. If you love God with all of you, your heart will find comfort and healing in Him should other love break your heart.

The commandments are for the benefit of humanity; God does not need them because He is immune to what affects us as human beings. The strength of a bond will always equal the intensity of its pain; the two are directly proportional.

When we become too attached to something, we unconsciously and unintentionally neglect some things. For instance, in most cases, when people are too attached to their dreams, careers, or even callings, certain areas of their lives, especially relationships with others, tend to suffer. When you love something deeply, it is only normal to be too attached to it. I was in a certain office one day, and on its wall hung these words, *"love without depending"*. I found these words quite interesting because, to think of it, God loves human beings, but He does not depend on them, so this, to me, implies that loving without depending is possible. Practising non-attachment, allowing what flows and accepting what does not, is only possible if you stop resisting certain things.

There are times when resistance can cause you pain. I remember a time when things were not going my way, and I reacted to that by being extremely busy so I could resist the moment I was in. It came as a revelation to me then that I should stop resisting what is and allow life to be. My situation had not changed, but I found myself engulfed in peace because I had ceased to be resistant to my temporary reality, which was only causing me frustration in return. Sometimes, peace comes when you eliminate the desire or need to change something and allow life to be. All that is part of life has its place in the universe, whether we define it as positive or negative.

Love, by its very nature, is somewhat possessive. It is common to hear possessive pronouns such as 'his, hers, ours, mine,' and so forth in romantic relationships to show how possessive love is. It is our duty and responsibility to monitor the possessiveness inherent in love. We were created and left with the responsibility of learning to master and shape ourselves. Look and acknowledge your possessiveness and let it go. It is in setting things and others free that we become free ourselves. In one of her poems, Dr. Maya Angelou speaks of love as liberating. If your love cannot liberate, it carries potential harm with it. Love, but add the ability to liberate in your love. At some point, you may have to part ways with what you love. If we were to make liberating part of our loving, separation would not be that painful and gruesome. Love ceases to be love and turns into something toxic when obsession and extreme possessiveness take over.

You become needy, desperate, and insecure, and all of these are highly unattractive in a relationship. Let us normalize loving people without owning them. The alarming rate of femicide is clear evidence of how much possessiveness has taken precedence over love. The danger with owning people is that when they do you wrong, you will feel justified to cause them harm.

Psychology clearly teaches that the one person you have control over is yourself. No matter how long you may be in union with another individual, that does not change the fact that the only person you have power and control over is yourself. The very fact that a person can do something you never expected of them in a relationship is a clear sign that you do not own their thinking, behaviour or conduct.

Some of the things that people do in relationships have nothing to do with the other but it has everything to do with who the person is. Own yourself fully, master yourself completely and be free from illusory entitlements and a sense of ownership over the other. Be so content in your own company that the presence of the other becomes a want. It is possible that Paul in the Bible led such a life of contentment in his own company.

Not having a solid sense of self is one reason why you may easily lose yourself in the midst of certain associations. People who are not afraid of their own company are the ones readiest to be in relationships.

In the book of Genesis, God said concerning Adam, "It is not good for a man to be alone". But, it is worth noting that Adam never said anything to God about his singleness; hence, to me, he does not appear to have been a man who was afraid of his own company. His contentment in his singleness qualified him for a suitable companion, which explains why he saw Eve as the bone of his bones and the flesh of his flesh. He never said anything about Eve completing a certain void in him. All he did was to affirm who Eve was in relation to himself (the bone of his bones and the flesh of his flesh), affirm her identity, how she would be known in the world (she shall be called Woman) and acknowledge her origin (because she was taken out of Man). Incompleteness sees incompleteness; emptiness sees emptiness, and completeness sees completeness. Adam saw Eve in light of his very own being, and the same principle still holds true today; we see others in light of who we are. Everything Adam said about Eve pointed back to himself.

It is an individual and personal responsibility to always mind the degree of our attachment to something. I once knew a man who loved his car so much that he never separated from it. Wherever he went, he used it even in places that were just a foot walk away; he would use his car. A day came when his car was broken; he became sour for days; that is just how attached he was to his car. Anything you are too attached to; without it, you are either miserable or nothing. That is why it is very important for people to be content with themselves first before they can seek anything external. The attachment is responsible for our seeking meaning in things that cannot be given to us. We become too materialistic but remain miserable and still feel that life is meaningless despite all we have acquired because we are unaware that we are looking for meaning in things that cannot be given to us.

We are loving what cannot love us back. Man-made things cannot love us back the way we love them. Anything outside yourself that you think you need to feel worthy, you should get rid of because that is just the ego talking.

Humanity is unaware of how it's bound by the chains of attachment; hence, it keeps complying without ever questioning. Anything you are unconscious of is likely to rule you, but the minute you become conscious, you set yourself free from many chains. Even change is resisted by our attachment to the old way of doing things. We become so attached to the familiar that we end up resisting the unfamiliar even if there is nothing wrong with the unfamiliar. When we are too attached to the old, we cannot accept and embrace the new. Even Jesus Christ was greatly resisted by the Pharisees for disrupting their norms, with which they were so familiar and comfortable. At times, you have to let go of who you used to be in order to allow who you are becoming to fully emerge. Somebody once said, "An excessive attachment to anything in life makes you mentally enslaved.

"Love without attachment is the purest love because it is not about what others can give you because you are empty. It is about what you can give others because you are already full."
– Unknown

3 | The Inevitability of the Attachment

It is not prevention but control; it is not in your power to acquire or not to acquire it, but it is in your power what you do with it. Like an invisible missile aimed at humanity, it will catch us all, but not all of us will be torn apart by it. It sets the heart and mind at war and causes the two to move in different directions. The heart yields to it without thinking, while the mind tries to assess it to see if it is worth entertaining. The choice it gives comes with so much agony; if you do not yield, you will be left wondering how it would have been had you yielded. Like two diverging roads, the one you take will make you wonder what the one you did not take is like.

With attachment, it is as difficult not to experience it as it is to make a choice. Even the most hardcore person does get attached, although he may not show it. This missile called attachment hardly misses its target: human beings. Mothers may cry when their only child, whom they are very fond of, has reached a stage of independence and must leave home. The feeling may be mutual for fathers, but they will not show it because they are supposed to be strong. The avoidance of the attachment is not necessarily its absence.

If you have a heart, you are bound to become attached to someone or something at some point in your life. It springs up from within in response to what the eye sees on the outside and before you know it, it has taken total control of your heart. It needs no verbal communication to develop, it is an energy that connects hearts. Although communication is important for maintaining it, it is not a prerequisite for initiating it.

Attachment is far beyond words and way greater than them. It may appear as if you have overcome it when the person or thing you were once attached to is out of sight, but should your paths cross at some point, you realize that there is still a residue of it that is left. Two people who were once married and divorced may need a change of environment and be far apart from each other to forget about each other. Simply because something is out of sight and out of mind does not necessarily mean it is no longer there; it means you have temporarily forgotten about it because you no longer see it as you used to. You can be shocked at times when you find yourself experiencing something when you thought you were long over it; hence, lovers who had been separated for a very long time can reconcile and be together again after a long period of separation. The attachment is inevitable in the sense that you do not choose it; it chooses you. The heart is said to be a wellspring of emotions; all forms of emotions flow from it, and no one can hide or run away from their emotions because they are a part of them.

In a movie called *Equilibrium*, emotions are deemed to be the most fatal human virus, and as a result, human beings in that area had to be completely stripped of their ability to feel. So, being without emotions means I can kill without mercy, listen to music but find no pleasure in it, and be in a relationship for the sake of meeting certain ends, not necessarily because I am in love with that individual. Being emotionless makes a man an island because he is attached to nothing but his own mind, and he is, at times, a master and, at other times, a servant of his own mind. There are times when we all feel that we are in control but there are also times when we feel that we are losing that control. Sometimes, you may fall for someone and easily brush off those feelings, but at times, they are hard to ignore; the more you try to silence them, the louder they shout, and the more you struggle to escape them, the deeper you sink. As much as love can be a choice, at times, it can be a response to feelings beyond one's control. It is a war you do not choose; the only things you can choose are your weapons.

Not everything inevitable is viable, but there are times when that which is inevitable is also viable. Not every attachment is worth entertaining, just as not every developing attachment must be ignored. Sometimes, you may lose a soulmate due to fear, and sometimes, you may find yourself trapped in a toxic relationship, struggling to detach from an abusive partner who only brings out the worst in you. There are hormones responsible for bonding in a living human being; we are designed to attach, although the attachment process will mostly occur by default. The sea sometimes crosses the boundary set for it by the Creator, and it causes damage to all the structures and landmarks near it. Anything natural can spiral out of control and cause damage, and even good intentions sometimes manifest as bad and wrong actions. Some people become attached and fail to detach when circumstances necessitate, allowing the attachment to turn into a bitter obsession. We do not plan to become attached; it just happens, and once it does, we must find a way to deal with it. Inevitability is not necessarily uncontrollable.

"You can avoid reality, but you cannot avoid the consequences of avoiding reality"

– Ayn Rand.

4 | The Attachment Paradox

"Cry, the beloved country, for the unborn child that is the inheritor of our fear. Let him not love the earth too deeply. Let him not laugh too gladly when the water runs through his fingers, nor stand too silent when the setting sun makes red the veld with fire. Let him not be too moved when the birds of his land are singing, nor give too much of his heart to a mountain or valley. For fear will rob him of all if he gives too much."

– Alan Paton

The above statement nicely summarizes what an attachment paradox is: you will always be imprisoned for fear of losing what you love the most. Hardly anyone exists without fear of losing what they love the most. Anything you hold on tightly to will always make you a prisoner of fear. Overexcitement allows us to enjoy what we have in the moment as if nothing will ever go wrong, but fear creates room for disappointment. Every positive emotion must be accompanied by a corresponding negative emotion. Fear is one of the negative emotions that often helps mankind in achieving self-preservation. You rarely think wrong about something or someone you love too deeply because thinking about them only triggers positive emotions that make you feel good. Yet, emotions are also tricky because the same emotion of love can turn into anger and bitterness under unpleasant conditions.

Some people become angry with themselves for loving someone who doesn't seem to deserve their love. However, I think, at times, what is interpreted as love is merely a costly attachment because love, by its very nature, is pure and very far from evil. You sometimes hear stories of cheating partners who would not stand to see their partner with someone else despite having ended the relationship with them. You wonder why that person cannot stand the sight of their ex with someone else, although they keep breaking their heart when they are together and they call it love; it is not love. It is an unhealthy attachment accompanied by possessiveness and a sense of entitlement over another.

Deep love leaves deep wounds when it stops flowing. Sometimes, the fear is so great that people completely avoid the attachment. It is not always the fear of losing what one is attached to, but at times, it's being afraid of what might go wrong during your attachment; what if things do not work out? What if this or that happens? Fear creates a paradox in any form of attachment. If you are in a relationship as a woman, you may be intimidated by the attractive women working with your fiancé or boyfriend. Personally, I am of the view that, at times, what appears as an insecurity in one may be a deep-seated fear of losing the other, which is not well addressed.

What many are unaware of is that we are looking for ourselves in what we are attached to; when a part of you is given to something, it is no longer yours but belongs to what you gave it to. That is why most of the time when people have been cheated on by their partners, the first question that comes to their mind tends to be related to their self-worth. "Was I not good enough? What does he or she have that I do not have?" Forgetting that not everything done by your partner has to do with you; much of what people do in relationships is about who they are, not necessarily you. People do not come into relationships as blank slates or, as John Locke puts it in Latin, *tabula rasa*, but each one comes with their own tendencies, habits and background, which will influence who they become in a relationship. When you look for yourself in something else, it controls your sense of self-worth. You are only as worthy as it says you are, and that is where the danger of not owning our worth comes in. We need to unlearn this notion of two halves, making a whole that is destroying people's self-esteem and sense of self-worth. With or without it, you have always been worthy.

What could be the possible solution to this paradox? Kahlil Gibran states, *"Love one another but make not a bond of love; let it rather be a moving sea between the shores of your souls. Sing and dance together and be joyous, but let each one of you be alone"*. It is possible to love without forming a bond. I personally know it from experience; I love people but hardly become attached to them. Loving without forming a bond is like being friendly without befriending. You can be friendly to people without necessarily being their friend. Oneness must be accompanied by individuality. Learn to enjoy your own company as much as you do that of others. Add a bit of independence in your interdependence; there is too much uncertainty in this life; if you become too immersed in someone, finding yourself after losing them might be a steep uphill. Though the fear that creates a paradox in attachment must never be allowed to rule, occasionally listening to it is wisdom.

Much of our lives are a paradox and duality. We have to be ordinary while doing the extraordinary, humble while manifesting greatness, and modest while impacting the masses. We have always been ruled by the principle of duality. It is Jesus Christ himself who teaches us to be harmless as doves but wise as serpents. Two seemingly contradictory qualities can and do coexist in one and the same entity. The attachment paradox is an age-old syndrome, as old as humanity itself. By our design, one might conclude that we are meant to accept both the bitter and the sweet. Even those two differing voices that are always talking inside of you, bringing you confusion when having to make a decision, are enough proof that you have always been a prisoner of duality and contradiction. The paradox is not new to us; we have always been living with it, whether consciously or unconsciously.

The mind is paradoxical by nature; the very thing you are told not to think about tends to be the very thing you find yourself thinking of. When the instruction says, 'thou shalt not', the mind says, 'thou shalt'. I remember attending a counselor's training at the South African Depression and Anxiety Group. One of the trainers demonstrated the paradoxical nature of the mind by saying, 'There is no such thing as a pink elephant'; he then proceeded to say, try not to think about a pink elephant, and ironically, that is exactly what we all thought and imagined. I have noticed from personal experience that the days when I climb my bed with hyper-intensity to fall asleep are when I take longer. But when I lie in bed listening to music, I doze off without even knowing when I did. Just as fear can bring to pass what one is afraid of, a forced intention makes what one forcibly wishes impossible, says Frankl.

This excessive intention, or hyper-intention, as Victor calls it, can be observed particularly in cases of sexual neurosis. The more a man tries to show his sexual potency or a woman her ability to experience orgasm, the less they are able to succeed. The mind operates in a very paradoxical manner; who can know it if not him who devotes himself to studying and understanding it? You become attached to someone who never seems to even notice that you are into them, and those feelings turn into resentment. You want to be with someone, but once they start giving themselves too much to you- you shut off and begin to withdraw, and you do not even understand why you react like that. Attachment is very complex and confusing; if not monitored and controlled, it can become dreadful. Sometimes you do, sometimes you don't. One moment, it's yes, the next it's no. You are hot, then cold, and you end up confused. Being human is an extremely complicated experience because we are very complex creatures.

Most of the time, the male children who grow up with resentment towards their fathers and too focused on not wanting to be like them ironically become exactly like them in behaviour and mannerism. This too is a paradox.

"You can value and care for things, but whenever you get attached to them, you will know it's the ego. And you are never really attached to a thing but to a thought that has 'I,' 'me,' or 'mine' in it. Whenever you completely accept a loss, you go beyond ego, and who you are, the I Am which is consciousness itself, emerges."

– Eckhart Tolle

5 | The Poignancy of Separation and Parting

"Detachment is an art of enjoying something while always being open to the possibility of losing it someday."

– John B. Bejo

The detachment process is painful. It leaves people crying and regretting. When people are in love and strongly bonded, it's only normal for them to enjoy their attachment as if it will last forever. However, challenges often arise that threaten the bond and make detachment necessary. In any bond you form, it is not always about having your expectations of the relationship fulfilled; sometimes, it's about simply being able to say that you once loved. There are times when participation is more important than winning. It takes time and energy to nurture and grow an attachment, whereas in detaching, time, courage, and maturity are needed. I imagine the pain conjoined twins feel when they must be separated, that tearing of the flesh so that each one can survive on their own is painful but necessary. That is exactly how the detachment process is: painful but necessary. The way an attachment ends determines the degree of pain it leaves on the individual. The pain of detachment is intensified by harsh separations and made bearable by well-communicated terminations.

Never disturb the detachment process by suppressing and denying the pain it comes with; covering the wound without first treating it does more harm than good. There are times when you must allow yourself to bleed in order to heal. Normally, if two people are in a relationship and a breakup happens, the one most hurt by the breakup often claims they no longer care; they are long over the other, knowing very well that deep down they still care and are hurt by seeing the other person with a new partner. If you are hurt by detaching from someone or something you dearly love, allow yourself to grieve while looking on the bright side; the greatest insight usually comes from pain.

Pain communicates to us in so many ways, teaching us to reflect on the most important things in life. It necessitates reflection and re-evaluation of things. A bleeding wound or sustained injury needs to be properly treated for it to heal and the same is true of emotional wounds; the appropriate psychological remedies must be applied for the individual to heal.

I am giving you the freedom to cry, take it and use it because you will most definitely need it in this world of unceasing uncertainty. Do not be ashamed to cry; you can express your pain. The best cure for emotions is expression. Sometimes, crying is the best vehicle to carry you through your pain, but it cannot do that if you are ashamed of it. Do not be ashamed of your failures; own them as you do your achievements. Not everything is about triumph; sometimes, the struggle is what you need the most. Do not allow the process of detaching to turn you into a bitter person because when your tears dry, life will move on. We become attached to so much, and yet we often fail to recognize the depth of our attachment until the moment of loss or separation arrives. Only then do we come to realize the extent to which we were attached to something.

In each one of us, there is a child that never grows despite how old we get, and in times of pain and distress, this child appears through vulnerability and confusion. There are times of being overwhelmed, feeling a sense of lost control and acting without applying much rationality. The child in each one of us often emerges during times of pain and distress. You are not weak for feeling overwhelmed. You are not weak for being vulnerable. You are not weak for losing control over certain things. It is part of being human. When you go through the different emotions and seasons, you are only being human.

Life shares many things in common with love. It has many disappointments, setbacks, rejections, and failures, yet people fear death and fight so much for their lives when they are on the verge of losing it, as if sweetness and beauty are the only things this life has to offer when there is so much bitterness it gives us. Never fear to attach simply because you took time to heal from a detachment; just avoid being too attached. Never lose sight of love's beauty and preciousness because of the hurts and betrayals you encounter in love. We all have a nature-imposed obligation to learn how to deal well with loss. It is wise to balance dependence with independence, togetherness with autonomy, and our need for belonging with solitude so that we do not completely lose ourselves during the detachment phase.

Death is one event where there is a permanent detachment from those that we love and hold dear in our hearts; hence, humankind will never get used to it. Imprisonment temporarily separates people from their loved ones, but even though the separation is temporary, it is never easy. Family members cry hysterically when their guilty loved ones are sentenced to many years in prison. Mothers often cry when they must release their children, who have grown old enough to start living their lives independently of them. In certain passages of the Bible, believers cried for Paul when he was leaving after having finished what God had sent him to do in that place.

Anything that involves separating or detaching is hardly, if ever, pleasant to a human being. The countless cases of bitter ex-boyfriends and ex-girlfriends serve as proof of how hard the detachment process can be. You hear of individuals who committed suicide or became depressed after their partner ended the relationship, and if you understand the pain of detaching from what you were attached to, you will not blame them. If the pain of losing something becomes overwhelming, always remember that there was a time when you did not have it, and yet you lived. If you did it then, you can most certainly do it now. If you had lived without it in the past, you could live without it in the present. Loss has a tendency to make us forget what we still have and what we can still appreciate, but each time we remember what has not been taken away from us, despite what we may have lost, we are able to bear the losses of life. In the Bible, Job had lost it all, but he still had his soul to be grateful for; he still had life to appreciate. Pause and think! What do you still have after all your losses? What is it that remains in spite of the ruins?

The best way to deal with the pain of separation is to acknowledge it because the more you deny and suppress it, the longer it will take to heal from it. Emotions are mysterious; the more we deny what we are feeling, the more we feel what we are in denial of. From his own personal experience of denial and suppression, *Abner Mariri* states, "Emotions do strange things to your head—if you do not give them space to breathe, they manifest in other ways. What I was suppressing was going to lead me down a path I never imagined myself on". We should normalize talking about what eats us on the inside without the influence of alcohol. Allow yourself to feel the pain, but do not feed the pain.

Times of pain and sorrow come unplanned and unannounced. We are all found trying to make life better and more fulfilling because the worst need not be much effort for it to happen, but the best takes a lot of effort to create. We are looking for remedies and strategies for this battle of life. I find it amazing that we have to be taught about the right ways of living, but we never sat in class for messing up. We seem to have been born into a mess that we spend most of our lives trying to fix.

Attachment is neither right nor wrong; the greatest mistake many of us make is engaging with things without first trying to understand how to handle their ups and downs. Not everything is meant to be learned by experience; life lessons are both within and around you. Tune in to yourself and listen to yourself; there is something you will learn. Look around you and listen to the stories of others; there is something you will learn without having to experience anything firsthand. Life always presents lessons to us if we are attentive enough to see them, but our narrowed scope of learning hinders us from seeing them because we are comfortable with our unimodal way of learning. As a result, we end up committing a lot of errors that we could have avoided and suffering pain that we could have spared ourselves.

To those who are hurt and bleeding inside because of previously held attachments, your pain will be former, just as the pleasure you once enjoyed. Eckhart Tolle, in his best-selling spiritual book entitled *"The Power of Now,"* speaks of being detached from the outcome when you do something so that you can enjoy the process itself and treat success and failure alike. Detachment is not all doom and gloom; by detaching from certain things, we spare ourselves a lot of pain and sorrow. It is through separation from things that we get to see the real magnitude of our attachment to them. I remember a time when my laptop was taken from me because I had not paid my rent as a tertiary student; it felt as if I had been separated from a part of myself as if a part of me had temporarily died during those days without my laptop. Threats to attachment serve the purpose of revealing the true intensity and depth of our attachment to things and people. Listen to what *Eckhart Tolle* has to say about our fear of separation as human beings:

"People tend to be uncomfortable with endings because every ending is a little death. That is why, in many languages, the word "goodbye" means "see you again."

Whenever an experience comes to an end—a gathering of friends, a vacation, your children leaving home—you die a little death. A "form" that appears in your consciousness as that experience dissolves. Often, this leaves behind a feeling of emptiness that most people try hard not to feel or face. If you can learn to accept and even welcome the endings in your life, you may find that the feeling of emptiness that initially felt uncomfortable turns into a sense of inner spaciousness that is deeply peaceful. By learning to die daily in this way, you open yourself to Life."

The process of detaching from someone or something is difficult and painful, but remaining attached even when you must let go is even worse. When you are afraid of nothing, you become free from everything. Therefore, be at peace with both the pleasure and pain of attachment. Sometimes, the pain is not directly from the detachment but from resisting it as part of life. Just as we accept attachment to certain things and people, we should also be careful not to condemn the detachment process when time and circumstance demand and necessitate it. There are times when the pain of separation is stronger and more fearful than death. Death ceases to be fearful when pain is stronger than it; hence, people often wish for death when in pain. When two pains meet, the lesser pain bows.

One of the greatest lessons that much of humanity is yet to learn is being able to sit courageously with your pain without avoiding any part of it and without hiding from its presence. The flight from the presence of pain often results in disaster as people end up engaging in harmful acts and detrimental behaviours to flee from their pain. Unexpressed emotions do not disappear; they lie low only to resurface afterwards. When you allow yourself to fully feel your pain, you are completely setting yourself free from it. Energy always flows to where the attention is; what you try to avoid the most is exactly that which you will get the most. Nicky Rowbotham tells us that what you focus on and pay attention to matters. She further adds that you should not give energy to what you do not want and then blame it for giving you what you do not want.

Pain can follow you like God followed Jonah if you try to flee from its presence. We cannot hide from our emotions; they are a part of us, and we need the wisdom to handle them accordingly. *Marianne Williamson* states that relationships and separation are beautiful and interesting. She says, "Relationships are eternal. The separation is another chapter in the relationship. Often, letting go of the old form of the relationship becomes a lesson in pure love much deeper than any would have learned had the couple stayed together". Separation is not all pain and gloom, but it can be a new chapter which comes with new ways of relating with your significant other.

It is only when we change our perception of an ending thing and draw the lessons it brought us that we can completely heal and let go with gratitude for all that we have learned from it. Endings do not always have to be bitter and painful because it is possible and doable to lovingly detach from something. You can keep your distance without being resentful; you can break up and still be civil to each other; it is called maturity; it is a child of wisdom. Is this not what God Himself is teaching us when He is found having a conversation with Satan, who rebelled against Him and even went to the extent of sealing deals with him regarding the very children of God? Harmonious endings are possible, especially when we are able to see the new beginnings that always follow thereafter. The heaviness of an ending is always followed by the lightness of a new beginning. There is power in not being attached. Hence, the enemy who has nothing to lose is the most dangerous enemy. I do not think that there is anyone who literally has nothing to lose, but when the mind is opened to losing as it is to win, loss and gain become the same.

"It is the tears that have got us through the darkest days and the hardest times. Many of us have been able to float on our tears to a new and better understanding of ourselves. Through our tears, we get in touch with those experiences that we have forgotten, hidden, or buried away in the pit of our souls"

– Iyanla Vanzant

6 | Memento Homo
(Remember You Are Only Human)

You delight in being loved, and you are hurt by being hated; it is part of being human. You love acceptance and resent rejection. That, too, is part of being human. Compliments exhilarate your spirit, whereas criticism wounds your ego that, too, is part of being human. Whatever is said about you, whether good or bad, affects you. Even though you try to pretend malicious rumors don't affect you, deep down, you know they do. That, too, is part of being human. All these things society teaches you to ignore—you know deep down they do matter. 'It doesn't matter what they say about me; it doesn't matter what they think of me or how they look at me.' Are these not the lies we tell ourselves? Oh, human? We often say, 'You can't be loved by everyone,' but the truth is, it would be nice, if we can be. Beneath criticism and condemnation lies a yearning for the very things criticized and condemned.

You are wired to love and be loved— that is why hatred hurts you. You are designed to be accepted; living with the opposite is something you learn; it is not innate in you. There are things we are wired to love. Should we not find them, we must learn to live without them; we have to learn to live without them. Sometimes, being human means learning to live without what you know, deep down, would make you happy. A child who grows up without love, attention, and affection learns to live without these things, but under normal circumstances, they would have loved to have them. It's not wrong to admit you've learned to live without it, but if it were possible, you would have loved to have it—that, too, is part of being human.

What is it that you deeply yearn for but you have learned to live without? Do not deny your human experiences; they are a beautiful part of you that is worth each and every appreciation and acknowledgement. I had to learn to live without my mother; I had to learn to live without my father; I had to learn to live without my sister and without unity in my family for some time despite my deeper yearning for peace and harmony within it. I've had my fair share of learning to live without things dear to me. In life, sometimes you can find yourself getting what you do not want before getting what you truly want. You will ask yourself and others what you could possibly be doing wrong. I have been there; I know it from personal experience. The taste of the unwanted, when what is wanted is known, is very bitter.

There are things that will break you before they make you because they are not part of your natural design. It is not easy for someone who has been in a happy and satisfying relationship for the longest time to be by themselves; before they can accept being by themselves as normal, there is some pain to pass through. I am of the view that certain things we do naturally, but some things we have to train ourselves to do. I have heard many stories of divorcees who never wanted anything to do with marriage after their divorce. When you listen to the stories of these people, you can tell that if things were different, they would still be happily married, but now, circumstances are forcing them to live without the things they love and desire the most.

When you say 'thank you' to a compliment, you acknowledge the effect another person's words had on you. If compliments warm our hearts, criticisms are bound to do the opposite. Even when you say you do not care, a part of you is somehow affected. You have no idea how simple and wonderful life becomes the moment we step into true authenticity with ourselves and our emotions. I remember a certain old woman who used to brag about how much people loved her. Each time I heard her bragging about that, in my heart, I would say, "But this is not something one can brag about, since human beings cannot be confirmed", but after some time, I came to realize that whether her being loved by people was a fact or opinion it really did not matter much, but it made her happy knowing that she is loved. She was being real about being human; knowing she was loved made her happy, and it goes without saying what the opposite would have done to her. Why are you bothered by what people say about you? Why is your ego bruised by criticism? Why is your soul downcast by rejections and negligence? It is all because you are only human, but you are somewhat made to be in denial of your humanness when it is so beautiful, precious and sophisticated. Stand in full honour and awe of your humanness to avoid denial of your human experiences.

Here, I want us to remember the fully human Jesus who wept, became hungry and became sorrowful and burdened. Here, I want us to reflect on the fully human Jesus who was not in denial of His human experiences but fully acknowledged them. The man who needed the support of His disciples in Gethsemane. The Jesus who fully felt the nervousness brought about by the hour of suffering. The Jesus who was tempted as we are and forsaken by God to be by Himself. Let us put the Son of God aside just for a moment and look at the Son of Man with all his experiences of being human and learn from him what it means to be authentically human.

He says to his disciples, "All of you will fall short of me tonight, and I will be left alone. Nonetheless, I am not alone, for my Father is with me". He first starts by saying He will be alone, that is, humanly or physically speaking. Yes, He was going to be alone, but He still found a bit of comfort that His Father would be with him. The book of Galatians says, 'those who are in Christ have crucified the flesh with its passions and desires' (Galatians 5:24-26). It is worth noting that crucifying the flesh is not the same as losing touch with our humanness. Jesus Christ perfectly models this in his life of total submission to God and His leadership while being vulnerable under certain circumstances, such as in Gethsemane. We are still very much in touch with our emotional side, and although we are spiritual, wisdom is needed to better handle our emotional side.

He cried but as somebody with hope. We often tell people not to cry, but the truth is that people should cry while keeping hope alive. Jesus was a man of sorrows, one acquainted with grief. Nonetheless, He kept His faith and trust in the Almighty God. His human experiences never shifted Him from God. On the contrary, they made Him rely more on God. Spirituality deepens our understanding of our humanness. It teaches us to listen to ourselves and pay attention to what our feelings and emotions are saying to us when they are saying it. There are days of going to bed with a broken heart and severe bruises to the ego, but daily, I am teaching myself not to be resistant to my emotional state, as fearful as it gets; I am learning to pay attention to what my reactions are saying to me about me. Changing how we relate to our emotions is a crucial part of our healing. Our emotions are messengers to work with, not against. We often miss the messages they bring because of how we've been conditioned.

I have healed some and wounded some. I was both an ointment and an ailment at the same time. I have been through difficult phases that needed me to make hard decisions, the kind that left other people crying. Everything, no matter how good it may be, has two sides to it. Over the years, I have struggled to be true to myself because of those who might be hurt in the process. I can't say I've fully mastered being authentic without worrying about how it affects others. My empathy, compassion and sensitivity have been both a burden and a blessing at the same time. Nothing has been as difficult as making decisions that left others hurt and disappointed, although I knew deep down that I had to make those decisions. There are things that are rationally good to do but emotionally draining to do. I know it because I have been there personally, and by the look of things, it is something I need to come to terms with because I am still going to experience it.

We have been through so much that we have not acknowledged it. We have been through a lot as humanity. We owe it to ourselves to appreciate our resilience. We have all had those moments where we wished what we heard was just a dream, and someone would come and tell us it was not true. We have all had our surreal moments that felt so unreal when they were so real. We have bled both privately and publicly. We have battled countless demons in our closets when nobody saw. We have had nights where our pillows were wet with tears, and nobody was close by to dry them. We have had to figure it out ourselves. We experienced failures and disappointments more than we could bear until the only choice we were left with was to be strong. We have been through circumstances that forced us to realize our resilience because we had no other choice but to be resilient. We cannot help but acknowledge and appreciate our human experiences and the resilience that carried us through it all. Some of you bear physical marks on your bodies for the things you survived.

You withstood the storm, passed the trial, and now you live to tell the tale. I appreciate you, oh dear human. My sincere desire and earnest prayer is that you may be completely free from this suffering. If I had it in me, I would deliver you from the distress in the blink of an eye. You are a part of me; I am you, and you are me. I am unable to ignore your pain, and your suffering greatly tortures me. I know, understand, and fully relate to the burden you are carrying daily on your shoulders. The war of a voice that you cannot silence in your head is a war of us all. This mind and this heart of ours have been through a lot. Sleepless nights, heartaches, depression and endless anxieties. If we were to be literally placed on bandages for all the emotional wounds we have suffered, I believe our bodies would be covered in bandages.

The unchosen whispers that we sometimes conquer and sometimes succumb to are in all of us. The twists and turns that sometimes leave us not knowing where to turn are common to us all. The masks we wear to keep life going, the emotions we suppress to go to work and the emotional luggage we have to bear with to put food on the table. The public pretences that haunt you alone in private. The identity crisis, inferiority complex, confusion and uncertainties of life we have been through. All of them are worth acknowledgement and appreciation as they form part of who we are. Someone once stated, *"You are sexual. You are soulful. You are emotional. You are spiritual. You are magic. You are human. Do not deny any aspects of who you are. A healthy soul is a whole soul"*.

We are a bitter, wounded, and bleeding generation because we have lost touch with ourselves. "I do not care" is a phrase that has become overrated. People get rejected, neglected, resented, hated, and unappreciated, and all they say is that they do not care. You hear them shouting in public, "It does not matter whether they love me or not; I do not care who they fall in love with after a breakup", yet deep down, care is always there, and it does matter whether they love you or not. I think we need to take a few steps back to disconnect from the lies we have been telling ourselves and reconnect with the true essence of our humanness, which is love and care. You are not a stone not to be emotionally affected by what happens to you. Acknowledge that you do care, and you lose nothing by admitting that you do care. If you live in denial of what hurts the most, you are also most likely to bleed the most. It is painful when people leave you. It is hurtful when people hate you. It is heartbreaking when people turn their backs on you. If really it did not matter, it would not hurt so much, would it? Acknowledge and admit that you are not weak; you are human.

In the garden of Gethsemane, Jesus Christ is quoted saying, "my soul is sorrowful even to the point of death". He allowed Himself to fully feel the sorrow and acknowledged it all without shame.

Sit and weep; some moments in life only need us to sit and weep. In Psalm 137, it is written, "By the rivers of Babylon we sat down and wept. When Nehemiah heard that the walls of Jerusalem were in ruins, he sat down and wept. Mary fell at the feet of Jesus and wept when her brother had died. Even Jesus Christ Himself wept. There is relief and healing through our tears. As we weep, we also wipe the pain away through weeping. Weep and wipe. We were designed to self-heal as human beings, and crying is one of the ways we heal ourselves. When we were born, we cried. When we were infants, crying was the only language we spoke. As infants, we communicated our needs through crying, and it worked. Why is it now that we have become ashamed of the very mode of communication that got us here? Crying brought us the needed rescue. Crying drew us the needed help. Become an infant once again and cry to the right people so that you may receive the help you most need. At times, the only thing that will carry you to the next day are your tears. You will have to cry it out in order to bear it through.

Let us learn from Jesus, who did not hide, avoid, deny, or resist what he felt when he felt it. As we stop hating the experiences that shaped us, we shall start loving ourselves more. We find ourselves in survival mode most of the time. We have so much to deal with. We have to be strong until we can no longer be. It is tiring to always be in survival mode. It is tiring to always have to endure. It is tiring to always have to be strong. There is dignity to our tiredness. There is a sacredness to our scares. We have been through the hard battles of life, having to forge weapons along the way as the battles deemed fit. There is no wound that will leave you without a scar.

There is nothing wrong with admitting that, indeed, you learnt something from the experience. Nonetheless, the price you paid for it was too high. Because indeed, at times, the experiences we learn through leave us with lifetime regrets. Our inclination towards negativity is very much understandable; the countless failures we have experienced left serious damage to our minds; hence, it's hard, if not impossible, as human beings to be completely without any fear of failure when contemplating trying something new. All the behaviours you are exhibiting have a source and point of origin; we accumulate a lot of psychological damage throughout our lives, and some of them we will never be able to solve in all our lifetimes.

You will get over some, and you will have to learn to live with some. It is our lot in this life as mere mortals. From dust, we were made, and to dust, we shall return, but not as we came, for God made us. Life has its own way of remaking us. We come whole and complete but leave fractured and wounded, for it is indeed, as Victor Frankl puts it, that in the past, nothing is irretrievably lost, but rather, on the contrary, everything is irrevocably stored and treasured. All that has ever happened to you, whether you remember it or not, is stored and treasured within you; none of it is ever lost. This, too, is part of being human. You will not be able to correct all the wrongs in your life, but if you are able to correct those wrongs, please correct them.

Do not accept who you are and what you can change about yourself. The fractured parts of yourself form part of who you are, but they are not who you are. In the book of John in the Bible, Jesus Christ makes a very profound statement when addressing the Pharisees. He says, 'Before Abraham was, I AM'. In other words, the true essence of who one is before all the experiences that one goes through. Before that rape, before that failure, before that divorce, before that sin, before those mistakes, before that heartache, YOU ARE. The essence of who you truly are in the sight of God was before you were, is after you have been and will always be after it has all been said and done. Before those life-changing experiences, you are. A fully God and fully human creature. What a wonder! Bishop Jackson Khosa, in one of his posts, once wrote, "When the winds of the Spirit begin to blow everything away, you discover your true self, the mystical 'I', the eternal 'I AM'. When you truly discover the 'I AM' in you- you enter heaven, you are out of hell. When you become aware of the 'I AM' in you, the mystical part of you that never left heaven in the first place is discovered. So in a sense, there is no need in the eternal 'I AM' to go to heaven, only an awakening, a remembering, a conscious awareness, an enlightenment". The true essence of who you are has never left you. It was only forgotten, and God is the very model and archetype of what you truly are: His image and likeness. Nothing can ever stop you from being the image and the likeness of God, and that is who you truly are. We sometimes hear of musicians who suffer speech impairment due to something tragic that happened to them, and they lose their voice, the only thing that they are known for. Do you see why it is important to understand your essence beyond labels? Labels can be lost, but who you truly are cannot be lost. The scripture says in Him we live, move and have our existence. That is where the true essence of our identity is found, oh dear human, in Him.

Muzi Cindi, in his book, beautifully sums up his call from God this way, "my call from God in Christ is simply a call to be everything I was created to be. It is a call to offer, through the being of my humanity, the gift of God to all people by building a world in which everyone can live more fully, love more wastefully and have the courage to be all that they can be. I see myself as a gift to the world and see each one of us as a gift to the world. That is how I live out the presence of this being we call God. I do not see this as a call to avoid pain, life's traumas and insecurities or to possess peace of mind. My God experience through Jesus is a call to be fully human, to embrace insecurity, loneliness, trauma, joy, peace, and restlessness. It is a call to experience God's presence and God's absence".

When a human life is open to all that humanity can be, humanity and divinity flow together as one, for at the depth of our humanity lies our divinity, declares Bishop John Shelby Spong. The more in touch we are with our humanity, the more whole we are, and the easier it becomes to manifest our divinity to the world. Only when one is whole and complete in themselves can one display the nature of God to the world. Our relationship with ourselves extends to God and others. He who is fractured on the inside will have a fractured view of God and the world. But to him who is whole and well, all things around him are also whole and well.

"Jesus never once in Gethsemane or elsewhere rebuked his emotions; he never once said, I rebuke this sadness, I rebuke this fear or get behind my emotions. Jesus was real about where he was and how he was feeling"

— Dr Anita Phillips.

7 | Association and Isolation

If association begets assimilation, what does isolation give birth to? A man of many companions reflects those companions, whereas a man of no companion reflects his unique individuality. Some individuals enjoy large social circles, while others, born more introverted, find comfort in their own space and company. There is a bond that is formed between associates, which may either strengthen or weaken over time due to several factors; destinations may differ, and life goals may require changes in environment, lifestyle, and letting go of previously held values.

Perspective is one aspect of association that makes it difficult to maintain because even with shared interests and values, it is bound to differ due to discrepancies in people's individual experiences and reasoning. People form collective identities through associations; when one fails, we all fail; when one conquers, we all rejoice. Association requires identification and connection but not physical proximity. One can identify and relate with a team they have only seen on television but have never met face-to-face. Such is the case with football fans and their favourite teams. People feel the pain of loss and joy of triumph as if they were physically there playing, too, when, in fact, they were just watching from a distance.

Whereas association is like joining a team that already exists, isolation is like building from scratch. Isolation is, for many, a reproach or resentment of some sort. When a prisoner is placed in solitary confinement, it is never because they have done something good, but as punishment for something wrong. In biblical times, isolation was mainly a result of being ritually unclean, such as in the case of lepers, women during their menstruation and so forth. So, human beings were created to form associations and connect with one another; hence, anything contrary to this brings some form of anguish. Only a few individuals can embrace solitude; most find pleasure in company and companionship.

In most cases, people who have isolation tendencies are usually the ones who did not have a good upbringing; they may have been either abused or neglected during their childhood. There is always a certain degree of agony that accompanies isolation. It is during times of distress that you hear people saying they want to be alone and think; hardly any happy person says that. It is in isolation that people get enough time and space to ruminate about their problems to the point of drowning in them. I believe we are born to connect with others; if you thrive in isolation, you must be a rare exception, as for most, it feels like a burden.

The association is closely related to inclusion, whereas isolation is a close companion of exclusion. You must be included before you can associate and excluded to be in isolation. Exclusion and inclusion are, to me, not opposite ends but rather two sides of the same coin with a serious overlapping effect. Your individual experiences can and do determine who you will be in a group, but who you alone always outlast who you are when with a crowd. You do not necessarily have to isolate yourself physically from people to be alone; you can even do it mentally by zooming in on the self while in the company of others.

I remember how lonely I felt as a tertiary student in my first year despite being surrounded by thousands of people within the university premises. You can detach mentally by wandering somewhere while physically in contact with someone or something. Association and isolation can both be either voluntary or involuntary. One can join social clubs out of their own choice or be obliged to interact with colleagues at work. Another can be alone by choice because they choose to be alone, or it can be a case of family members being on vacation somewhere and due to work they had to stay behind and be by themselves.

Humankind enjoys the pleasure of associating but is greatly hurt by the pain of rejection and isolation. When he forms social connections, he is, in fact, acting by the principle of where he comes from, for he was created to exist in unity. His Creator spoke in the plural and said, '"Let us make man in our image, after our likeness". Therefore, by rejoicing in association and resenting isolation, he upholds the principle by which he was created, the way he was designed to function and operate. Association is power. It matters who recommends you. Who vouches for you matters. Eckhart Tolle's book is said to have sold about 3000 copies after its release. After Oprah

Winfrey recommended it in her magazine column, the sales went drastically high. It matters who recommends you.

Human beings have an innate or inborn need for connectedness. It could be connectedness to God, each other, nature, the universe, or anything that could give them a sense of belonging. Relationships and bonds are formed in response to our need for connectedness to something. It is how we were created and designed to function. Although this proves to be costly at times, it is just how we were meant to function as human beings. From time to time, we associate and isolate. We form associations, but if they prove to be harmful or toxic, we isolate ourselves from them. Life thrives on balance; hence, everything must be balanced. There should be a balance between autonomy and togetherness, balance between individuality and collectivism and so forth. Let everything be balanced; too much of anything has never been good. Pain and distress have some isolation tendencies. People isolate and shut themselves off from the people who can be of help to them when in distress. It is through isolation from others that pain and distress kill and bury people.

"Never get too attached to someone because attachments lead to expectations, and expectations lead to suffering".

– Unknown

8 | Need For Belonging and Acceptance

One man once said, "No man is an island". Our need for a sense of belonging demands that we belong to a certain group or unit. The fear of being alone or rejected is sometimes what causes us to compromise ourselves. I sometimes sit by myself and ask, 'Why did things have to be this way?". We are such prisoners of our own senses and visibility. Have you ever thought of who you could be if you were invisible? Would you be the same person who is now doing the same things you do? Even though we may easily say that it does not matter what they say or think, deep down, we know very well that there is a part of us that cares. In one's life, there is room for another.

As human beings, we are part of a huge and endless cycle of interconnectedness and interdependence. We are born into families; we make friends and seek out relationship partners. Even the most emotionally cold and socially withdrawn of individuals will, to a certain extent, comply with the need for belonging and social acceptance by having his or her own small circles of friends, companions, or acquaintances. Hence, you find that even the most heartless people in history had small circles of people they considered friends or confidants. After it has all been said and done, everybody must have a social circle of belonging. It is as somebody once stated, *"You come to this world through someone, you are given a name by someone, you are raised by someone, at school, you are taught by someone. None of us is a product of our own selves"*.

My observations and experiences persuade me to believe that the need for belonging is something innate in us. I have often observed how strange it is when a man or woman stays alone and is never visited by anyone. We find it strange to the extent that we make unfounded speculations simply because he or she appears to be an island on which none of us lives according to our norm of living. Many experiences are more enjoyable when shared. Movies, for instance, are often more engaging when watched with others, sparking discussion and connection. It is natural for us to want to share both the good and the bad times with others, more especially the good.

The need for belonging cannot be separated from social acceptance. We easily find a sense of belonging where we feel welcomed. These two are as costly as they are beneficial. They torture loners with feelings of exclusion, which has resulted in many sacrificing and losing their true selves just to gain them. They make being different a reproach and fitting in a blessing. To be one's true self amid people of different values is way harder than finding a needle in a haystack. Many have succumbed to peer pressure, abandoned their values, and turned against their beliefs just to be accepted by others. The cost of belonging and acceptance can be as high as the sacrifice of true authenticity.

It is only natural to settle well in a group when similar values, shared ideas, and common interests facilitate common ground. We feel safe and secure when attached to individuals of similar thinking. So, to seek belonging is to seek a place where the inner self can be expressed without fear of opposition and criticism. When we say we seek belonging, we unconsciously say we need a safe space for self-expression to extend that within individuals who resonate with us. The need for belonging is an extension of the self to selves of the same kind. I feel free and happy when with people who are creative and spiritual like myself because in them, I see myself, and it feels normal to be the way I am. They become the echoes of my inner voice. The need for belonging and acceptance is normal and natural, but it needs to be guarded with caution because if not, it can lead to disaster.

Many people compromise their individuality just to fit in. Young people tend to be victims of peer pressure because of this need for acceptance and belonging.

A certain young man from Cape Town who used to be a top performer at school ended up turning into a gangster because, as a well-mannered and disciplined learner, he felt like an outcast in his community, where education was not valued, but gangsterism was the norm. He went all out to prove himself to the gang while losing himself in the process.

Such is the predicament of many, if not all of us. We all fall victim to conformity at some point in our lives. We just differ in our degree of it. It is essential to recognize that we are already part of humanity's vast family. The belonging we seek is ours—we simply need to awaken to it.

"Belonging belongs to you. You must have a fundamental belonging that is not predicated on anything external. You must first belong to yourself before you can seek to belong anywhere else."

– Rev. Angel Kyodo Williams

9 | Beyond the Separation Illusion

If you truly rejoice with those who are happy, most likely, you will also genuinely weep with those who are mourning. If you share in another's joy, you will most likely share in their sorrows too. That, in hindsight, is what I call the burden of interconnectedness. You can never be free from being part of the whole family of humanity. Even those who boldly assert themselves, despite what people say, still impact others in so doing. One can never be free from being connected to other human beings like themselves, whether they are aware of it or not. Human beings are deeply connected to each other in an extremely amazing way. Have you ever conceived an idea and kept it to yourself, only to see someone you have never shared it with implement it? That is just how interconnected we are.

The suffering of your kind is your very own. Their joy is your joy. People become very sad and angry when their favourite team loses a game, as if there is something tangible they would gain if it won. Whereas if it wins, they rejoice as though they were the ones playing when they were just watching. The attachment is responsible for the pain they feel from the loss and the joy they feel over the victory of their favourite team. There is no total freedom in attachment and connectedness. Johnny Clegg, in one of his songs, speaks about a strange freedom where he is only free to choose his chains. Due to connectedness, we cannot be completely free from each other; we just choose who we direct most of our attachment to. We are only free to choose our chains and who we tangle them with. Those who are barren greatly wish they could conceive, while those who have given birth have their own parental challenges to deal with. We are somehow always choosing our hard.

It is hard either way; you just choose which hard you can bear. It will cost you anyway; you just choose which costs are worth it. We always choose between steps; just make sure your step is worth the walk. Some are unhappy because of what they wish to have, whereas others are sad because of what they have. What, then, is the difference between those who have and those who do not if the possession of the former and the deprivation of the latter equally subjects them to pain? Whatever you choose, just know there will always be pain and suffering. It seems to me that, as far as life is concerned, humanity can never be completely free from existential suffering. As long as a human has the heart and mind, suffering will always be somehow created. Even inventions that were created with good intentions somehow contribute to death, disruption and corruption of life.

Compassion and empathy result from human interconnectedness. The distress you experience when someone passes on is a sign of our interconnectedness. The way the suffering of others moves you into humanitarian acts is also another sign of our interconnectedness. Throughout history, we see a long list of heroes and heroines who sacrificed their lives, their joy, their comfort, and luxury for the sake of others: Mother Teresa, who embodied and epitomised compassion; Florence Nightingale, who looked after the sick; Siddhartha Gautama, who left the luxury of the palace and a very beautiful wife in search of answers to human suffering and the long list of revolutionaries and freedom fighters who were bothered by the oppression of one by another. All these mentioned examples point only to one thing: that humanity, at its core, is deeply interconnected.

You do not need to be in pain to feel pain; through mere observation of another's pain, you already feel it. I am reminded of a preacher who once preached a sermon entitled, *"I am not the one who is sick, but the ache is mine"*. One of the ironies of being human is seeking connection when we are already connected. The book of Acts 17:27-28 states, "God wanted them to look for Him and perhaps search all around for Him and find Him, though He is not far from any of us". He wanted them to look and search, although He has never been really far. When you seek, it is because what you seek is already seeking you. The desire, the seek, and the search serve as evidence that something already exists and is within reach.

Compassion and empathy are no easy burdens to bear; I doubt there is anyone with an excess of the two who would enjoy life because their heart would always be with those who are suffering. It does not surprise me that some health workers lack these two qualities, especially some nurse. Imagine the number of sick and wounded people they are exposed to on a daily basis and think how overwhelming it would be to have to feel the pain of each patient or sufferer as though it were their very own.

I am a sensitive, compassionate, and empathetic person, but over the years, I have had to learn to control these qualities because an excess always made me want to save the whole world, which is impossible. I had to come to terms with my human limitations and open a room for loving the world as it is instead of always wanting to change and improve it. All things were given to us freely, but we must manage and monitor them lest they cause us to spiral out of control. Even if their qualities are good, because of the world we live in, they still need to be monitored well.

You may not be the one who is sick, but the ache may still be yours, too. There is no freedom in attachment; there is no liberty in connectedness. You are stripped of yourself while being yourself. Human beings live with each other without even noticing it. They live for each other no matter how much they try to live for themselves. We usually hide our pain, hurt and disappointments from our loved ones because we know very well how devastated they would be if they were to know what we are going through. Our hurts are painful to us, but they are even more painful to our loved ones.

There was once a lady who was going through a rough patch in her life due to marital issues, and she shared with me that her mother was more devastated than her for what her daughter was going through. The relationship crisis was terrible for the daughter, but for the mother, it was even worse. You would swear the ordeal was the mother's, yet it was her daughter's, but it tore the mother apart more than the daughter who experienced it first-hand. We are each other, whether we are aware of it or not. I never understood back then when one man said, *"You are another me, and I am another you."* But now, as I am delving deeper and deeper into the subject of attachment and interconnectedness, it is becoming clear to me what he meant by this statement. We are bruised as individuals, but we bleed as a crowd because of our interconnectedness. The late Dr. Maya Angelou saw this interconnectedness when she wrote, "I *come as one, but I stand as a thousand*".

I was so amazed to find myself drawn to a certain American spiritual teacher and author, only to realise that we share the same day and month of birth. Before realising that we share the same day and month of birth, I had been greatly and deeply drawn to his teachings. His wisdom and outlook on life resonated so much with me. While I was on that, another South African spiritual teacher and author whom I was so drawn to happened to be a twin like me and had a strong foundation of the Bible like myself. I marvelled at the similarities between these authors and myself. I then came to realise that they were another me, and I was another of them. One day, I was watching a video where Oprah Winfrey was interviewing Caroline Myss, and I was perplexed when Caroline Myss shared her opinion on death, which was like my opinion of death. It was on that day that I realised that I am connected to the deep and great wisdom of spiritual teachers and enlightened beings.

Have you ever noticed that somewhere out there, someone you have never met in person sees things the way you do? It is for this reason that we find ourselves drawn to certain individuals just by what they write and speak without necessarily having a close or personal relationship with them. Sometimes, you may speak or write something that was once spoken or written by someone without having seen it prior to speaking or writing it, and you may even feel that you are the first to grasp that observation or insight, whereas there are those who have seen it before you. Our interconnectedness accounts for such occurrences. We share things consciously and unconsciously as human beings.

To those who read the Bible, you should be familiar with the story of Peter being called by Jesus Christ to walk on water. By faith, Peter walked on water, and when he became afraid and doubted, the sea drowned him (Matthew 14:29-31). Now, the million-dollar question in this story is how the sea knew that Peter was doubting for it to drown him. Because there are no recorded words of Jesus telling the sea that Peter is doubting, he drowns him. Who tells the ants to come when you leave food crumbs on the floor? Who tells the weeds to take over when a land that was once used is no longer used? How many gifts and characteristics did you inherit from your bloodline? All the questions I am asking in this paragraph serve the sole purpose of showing you how connected creation is.

When the Lord Jesus Christ was teaching his disciples how to pray in what has come to be known as the Lord's prayer, He started by saying, *"Our Father"*. The statement is plural whether you are praying alone or as a group. He never taught us to be selfish; perhaps He knew that one lives for himself, but what happens to one, directly or indirectly, affects another. Divinity attests to our interconnectedness. The presence of the word 'our' in the opening line of the Lord's Prayer clearly shows that the self has been transcended and the other has been included in whatever is said afterwards. In praying by myself, the whole of humanity is affected and impacted.

You already have the connection you are searching for; you are unaware of it. You are connected to the creator, to humankind, and nature. Is it not wonderful to see that you are not as alone as you think you are? Our connectedness is very deep. I listen to songs sung in languages I don't even understand, but something in me just resonates deeply with them despite not understanding them. The connection of creation is beyond language and words. One of the greatest philosophers to ever live by the name of Jean-Paul Sartre, once said, *"Fashioning myself, I fashion the whole of mankind"* There is nothing you do that can just be about you, no matter how much you want it to be only about you. Even that which begins with you will not end with you. In empowering and developing yourself, you are also empowering and developing others because we are just as interconnected as that.

The wound may be yours, but the pain is ours. Blood is not always thicker than water, and I am sure by now you may have noticed that, but thank God for the connection to all that is; you now know that even if your own blood can desert you, you can never be disconnected from the larger family of humanity and all that is created. You are a partaker in another's pleasures and pains. Do not look at another's suffering as though it is us and them; if it happens to one, it shows that it can also happen to another. We are not isolated from the common suffering of mankind, nor are we separated from her joy. This belief in physicality and separation is the reason why we become jealous of another's success; we do not see it as ours. This belief in us and them is the reason why a person can be mugged while we look and do nothing. Move beyond this illusion to the true connectedness that exists between what is created.

According to the Bible, all became sinners because of one man, namely Adam and all were redeemed and justified from sin through the death of one man, namely Jesus Christ. We did not have to eat the forbidden fruit of us to be sinners; neither did we all have to die on the cross for our sins to be forgiven. It was one man who infected the whole earth with sin, and it was one man who redeemed humanity from sin. We suffered because of one man's deed, and we were liberated from sin because of one man's deed. Through Adam's disobedience, we all became sinners, and through Jesus Christ's obedience, we were all justified.

He who performs certain deeds does not perform them for himself only but for the rest of humanity because we are as interconnected as that. Even the scriptures themselves attest to the interconnectedness of humanity, as evident through the repercussions of Adam's disobedience to humanity and the benefit of Christ's death for humanity. We do not have to do it all of us; the one who acts for the whole of humanity. In the Old Testament, there are many people who died because of an individual's sin. It seems as if, even in the sight of God, humanity is an interconnected entity. When one who represents a certain group does wrong, the whole tribe is guilty.

I find it interesting how, as Africans, we relate to each other through clan names and similar surnames. Whether I know you or not, whether we come from the same family or not, if we share the same surname or clan name, we are automatically related. We are connected beyond blood. You cannot even marry someone with the same surname as you despite not being from the same family or bloodline. Because our surnames or clan names are similar, you cannot marry that person no matter how much you love them. As a child, I never really looked deep into this, but as an adult, I now see something worth noting and pointing out regarding our interconnectedness. You could have been born in one province but be related to someone in another province all through the mere sharing of a surname or a clan name. There is not much of a distance between humanity. You are part of me, and I am part of you. Do not be confused by the physical distance; we are connected, albeit the distance.

As an individual, you are a thousand in one. It now makes sense to me why some of the doctrines of the East assert that the "I "is an illusion and there is no such thing as "I." They say when we heal ourselves, we heal seven generations before and after us. There is nothing you do solely for yourself. Generations tied to you are affected when you do something. Being always conscious of such truths will make us cautious of our behaviour and actions. Some of what children are publicly are what the parents are privately. Inheritance is bitter and sweet at the same time. It does not filter which traits to transfer; hence, we inherited both good and bad traits from those who gave birth to us.
In the Bible, King David sinned because of a woman. Later on, his son Solomon turned away from God because of women. The father sinned because of one woman, and the son's heart turned away from God because of many pagan women. The fate of the father not only repeated but also multiplied itself upon the son. Sometimes, it may be asked, "Who did the child take after with such an evil heart when the parents are such good people?" But then you will discover that they received it from them. It's just that they will know how not to allow the dark trait to control them. Have you ever noticed the power and mystery of an introduction? Have you ever noticed that when you become introduced to someone you never knew before, your chances of meeting them again are increased? There are people I was introduced to in my area either through

work, a friend or through a particular event. After having known them for the first time, I started bumping into them more often now that I knew them than I did when I did not know them. It appears to me as if the invisible force of connectedness in human beings always lies dormant, waiting for an opportunity to be introduced; after that, it takes over, creating countless opportunities to bump into the same person you were introduced to. When you are introduced to someone, not only is your name, occupation, gender, or status introduced, but paths become intertwined; hence, they keep crossing each other more often.

When I am introduced to you, I am introduced to all that makes up you, visible and invisible. It should not come as a surprise why some people can connect during their first encounter and why others can clash during their first encounter without knowing much about each other. Apart from knowing my name and recognising my face, there is a communication between our auras. During my first year as a tertiary student, something was happening that I was paying close attention to: whenever I queued either for food or for a bus, the person standing either behind or in front of me would be a Christian. The way in which this occurrence repeated itself, you would swear I was the one planning it, but I did not. I exchanged numbers with a couple of people I met in queues because when I engaged with them, I would come to realise that we were speaking the same language of the Christian faith. Similar frequencies attract each other; your spirit knows its kind and cannot be deceived.

You represent thousands tied to you by the common bond of humanity. It is a common bond because it connects you to all who are common to the family of humanity, whether pleasurable or painful. Hence, Paul says in the book of Corinthians, *"Nothing has overtaken you except that which is common to all of humanity."* You are not exempted from all that is common to humanity because you are an inseparable part of humanity. Suffering and pain connect us as much as they wound us. They are the common threads running through our stories and different human experiences. Dr. Jean Houston states, "The *universe is one great quantum reality where everything is related to other things."*

The lowest form of consciousness is what he calls the *"ego consciousness"; it* is the time when we believe that who we are is our bodies, what we can do, what we have and what people think of us. The second form is *"group consciousness"*, which is a bit higher than the ego consciousness but still causes problems. It identifies with groups, which can create enormous wars and conflicts. The "Us" and "them" kind of consciousness. The third, which is also the highest form of consciousness, is what he calls *"unity consciousness"*. In this level of consciousness, we see ourselves as connected to each other, and when we see the other human being, we see the unfolding of spirit rather than appearance. In the unity consciousness level, competition is replaced by cooperation; when you see another human being in pain, you know that a part of you is in pain.

We ought to shift from the ego consciousness to the unity consciousness in order to understand how connected we are and honour that connectedness that exists between us as we should. Unity consciousness is the reality of who we are. Martin Luther King further emphasises it this way, "In a real sense, all life is inter-related. All men are caught in an inescapable network of mutuality, tied in a single garment of destiny. Whatever affects one directly affects all indirectly. I can never be what I ought to be until you are what you ought to be, and you can never be what you ought to be until I am what I ought to be. This is the inter-related structure of reality".

Terence states, "*Homo sum, humani nihil a me alienum puto*", which, when translated, means, "I am human. Therefore, nothing human can be alien to me". One of the pearls of wisdom I have come across in my life taught me that the different personalities we come across in our lives represent certain aspects of ourselves. In light of the fluidity of individual identity, this statement made a lot of sense to me. What is explicit or clearly seen in one person could be secretly harboured in the heart of another.

Most things, if not everything, are a reflection of what you are. If we saw nothing human as being alien to us, doing unto others as we would love to be done to us would not be a problem. Whatever you do to another, you do to yourself because of our connectedness. I do have my differences as a person, things I do not agree with, but I always try to honour the sacredness of humanness by seeing every individual first as a human being before I can look at them as either male, female, religious or non-religious. It is only when we fully honour the sacredness of being human that we can be able to reach out to other human beings in a spirit of love, care and compassion. There is healing from our individual and collective wounds when we fully align with our oneness as humanity. Some scars have been left by rejection, seclusion and marginalisation of people from the whole, but as we step into this dimension of interconnectedness, humanity will be healed.

When you fully understand our interconnectedness as human beings, you will also understand why minding one's business is difficult for many. No matter how much you try to ignore all else and focus only on yourself, somehow, you will find yourself bothered by what is happening in the lives of others, by how they live their lives, by what is happening in their lives and what they do with their lives. I think what we call being nosy is a trait that communicates something that is often overlooked in our nature as human beings. But up until now, we have not received the message, and the message is that of interconnectedness.

Something in us has always been telling us that humanity is one large family, but because we did not know how to decode the messages sent to us, we missed them. Even that which you label as negative carries a message; only if you listen and pay attention will you hear.

Interference is also an aspect of our interconnectedness. We are either moved or bothered because a part of us is doing something. Perhaps this will change your view and make you more tolerant of people who always meddle in the affairs of others. You are me, and I am you. I would only be deceiving myself if I were to pretend as if I am not concerned or worried about you. You are an integral part of the whole. We hardly talk about the heaviness that comes with having to cut people off because it was the only choice we had left for the preservation of our inner peace and sanity, yet it does occur. Without holding back, let me boldly admit, "YES, I DO CARE", and I lose nothing by admitting to that.

"The only problem you have is a belief that you are separate from God. The belief is that I am separate from you; you are over there, and I am over here. Gays are separate from straight; Whites are separate from Blacks. The belief in that illusion and physicality makes me think I can do anything to you. Every time I show up, I am a representation of past and future generations because of our oneness."

– Iyanla Vanzant

10| False Hope Hurts

"Hope deferred makes the heart sick, but when the desire is fulfilled, it is a tree of life"

— Proverbs 13:12

You may have heard many things about hope: *hope does not kill, hope does not disappoint, hope should not be lost* and so forth. Yet, there are times when hope hurts. If you have ever taken care of a sick loved one you hoped would recover but did not, you can understand what I mean when I say there are times when hope hurts. If you have ever tried to rekindle a spark in a dying relationship that eventually died, you will better comprehend what I mean when I say there are times when hope hurts. When two people are joined or bonded by love, expectations and goals come with being in a relationship. Some are conscious, while others are unconscious, and they only surface to awareness when the union comes to an end. Hope keeps the mind fantasizing about things desired, even when the desire proves to be unattainable.

I once read a very interesting story of a beggar who stayed in the streets without warm blankets but was resilient enough to withstand the extreme colds. One day, a man came by and promised to bring him warm blankets the next day, but he did not fulfill his promise. When this man who had made a promise to the beggar went to check the beggar, he found that he had been admitted to hospital due to extreme cold. When he asked this beggar how and why he survived the extreme weathers all along till the time he came to him promising to bring him blankets, the beggar said, "when you promised me blankets, my mind loosened its defences against the extreme weather conditions because it knew the blanket was coming".

False hope killed this beggar. The mind had adjusted and adapted to his living conditions until he was promised change that never took place. The resilience of mentally disturbed homeless people is a mystery to me; they eat from dustbins and sleep on the streets but hardly get sick. From a psychological viewpoint, I think this is something worth noting because we might learn something from it. There is a lesson in everything, and if we are attentive enough, even insanity can teach us something. We should ask ourselves why is it that those whose minds are no longer in a state to rationalize and overthink things seem to excel in resilience.

Could it be that much of humankind's sorrow and reduction in resilience is from hope that never became a reality? This is a question you can ponder yourself and answer as honestly as possible. Does not hope for a better future at times make the present suffering unbearable? Doesn't wishing to be elsewhere sometimes intensify the pain of where you are now? Where does much of our distress originate from? Are they not a result of being here but wanting to be there? Hope is for the future, which to some extent detaches us from the present. When we are detached from the present, we cannot fully enjoy life because we are absent from the only moment we are certain of. Hope for the future should be balanced with appreciation of the present.

No matter how temporary many things are in this life, every human being has a subconscious desire for permanence and eternity. It should not come as a surprise that up until today, neither of us has fully come to terms with death despite it having been in existence for many generations. Our subconscious desire is a desire for permanence with all that we are attached to and that which we treasure the most. I remember a certain lady who lost her lover of six years through a car accident; what she told me was that her prayer was for them to be together forever and that there should be none between them who died before the other.

But unfortunately, the opposite happened, and she was left devastated. Human beings have a desire for eternity in their mortality. Divorces and breakups are not the direct cause of people's pain; rather, it is often this unconscious desire for permanence that causes real pain. You are not wounded directly by the breakup but by your desire for permanence with what you are attached to. Have you ever taken time to ask yourself why you respond the way you respond to things? If you did, you would have discovered a lot.

Many human responses to the external world are not innate or natural. Instead, they are learned responses. Why are you devastated by failure? It has a lot to do with how, from an early age, you were treated for having failed and how you would be rewarded for passing and be punished for failing. I wonder what would happen in a world where people were taught that, at a certain stage of marriage, you must divorce; at a certain stage of a relationship, you must terminate it. I wonder if our responses and reactions to the detachment process would be the same. When soldiers in a war kill their opponents, it is victory calling for a celebration, but if an ordinary citizen kills someone, they are burdened by their conscience because they have committed a punishable crime. What determines the different responses in these two cases is largely the rules governing each one more than anything, it's nurture (environment) over nature (biology). What guides the response of the soldier and the ordinary citizen is what they were taught, which in turn has an impact on their consciences based on the nature of the teaching.

We generate our responses to things by ourselves, but because we have not come to a clear understanding of ourselves, we do not see things that way. The expectations and hopes with which you form an attachment become the very cause of your pain and disappointments. It is common to hear people in relationships saying, so and so will change; time goes by, and the person never changes. Some are abandoned by partners they still deeply love, and out of love, they keep hoping their partner will come to their senses, though sadly, this doesn't always happen. And those are the moments when hope hurts, my dear friends. I hope we can keep a film that has ended up playing. Hope sets people in a bargaining mode, imagining how things might have been if circumstances were different. Hope keeps us praying for the return of people who have fully made up their minds about leaving us. It is hope that hurts.

It makes it hard for people to detach; some even go to the extent of playing seers just to comfort themselves. You hear people saying, 'I know he or she will miss me' even though they're unsure; deep down, they hope it will happen. With each difficulty in detaching from what or whomever, there is also a deep-seated hope that things will turn for the better, and at times, the very hope for the better becomes the very cause of bitterness. That is hope when it hurts. I once said to someone, 'Hope does not kill', and he responded to my statement by saying, "Indeed, hope does not kill, but at times it does disappoint". I had never seen it that way before, but when he mentioned it, it resonated deeply with me, as I bear testimony to this truth myself. Though you may not die for hoping, but that hope will not always deliver what you hope for. If we were to adopt this truth as our very own, we would know when to let go and experience less pain in doing so.

Have a special appreciation in your heart for the usually resented things of life. Appreciate the lessons you got from your pain, appreciate the insights from your losses and the gifts from your groans. Pain can be either a blessing or a curse; it all depends on how you look at it. Your wails have wonders, and your groans have gifts for you. If you would look carefully, you would see the silver lining accompanying every dark cloud. To fully say yes to life means to fully accept and appreciate all that is part of living.

When you set yourself free from wanting to change how life works, you become free indeed. We are governed by the principle of duality, the law that necessitates pairing of all that is, pros and cons, light and darkness, freedom and bondage and so forth. None of us is free from this principle of duality; we are all bound by it. Unconditional appreciation is a must if humanity is to move to a level of being happy and satisfied with life. Be able to appreciate life as it is despite it being not as you would want it to be. Unconditional appreciation begets unconditional acceptance of all that is.

Be grateful for the pain that enabled you to better understand the pain of another. Be grateful for the suffering that helped you to develop more empathy towards humanity. Be grateful for the tragedy that transformed you for the better. Appreciate unconditionally and be grateful continually; as you do, you will begin to see a whole new world. When you begin appreciating the unpleasant, the unpleasant will begin to appreciate you, and when the unpleasant appreciates you, it ceases to be unpleasant to you. In showing his appreciation of the unpleasant, Friedrich Nietzsche said, *"I do not suffer from insanity; I enjoy every moment of it"*. To endure or to enjoy is a choice. You can suffer from or get bliss from it; it is all up to you, and the power to choose is always within you.

Cracked walls are the ones that let in light, and God is said to be close to the broken-hearted. In view of this, it should not come as a surprise why there should be some appreciation for pain and why some of those who are enlightened see pain as a gift. Who wouldn't appreciate an experience that launches them into the divine? Even the spiritual awakening for many it begins with some tragic event that forces them to look at life and themselves in a completely new way.

Muniba Mazari had a terrible accident that left her wheelchair-bound, but today, she is impacting people's lives in a massive way. Many other individuals went through nerve-wracking experiences, and because of those experiences, today, they know what matters the most in life.

A certain degree of pain, distress and tragedy is always involved in moving us from superficiality to finding the true meaning of life. In times of happiness and excitement, there is little to no time for reflecting on the most important things in life. Pain and suffering are the two masters who always launch us into the deep. Even when you read the Bible, you will realize that the Israelites repeatedly turned away from God when things were good, and calamity was always needed to turn them back to Him. Pain and suffering are not all bad; there are things we discovered because of them that we would not have without them. The Bible, in the third chapter of Ecclesiastes, tells us that everything under the sun has its time.

There is time for love; there is time for hatred. There is time to be born and time to die. Therefore, if everything has its time, it means everything must be made manifest in this universe. Whether it is pain or pleasure, it must be made manifest, and it will mostly manifest through human beings. Life thrives on balance. Good times and bad times should balance each other. It is the happy moments that become your therapy during dismal days. Previous happy moments are therapeutic in nature; they remind us that life can still be better when we are surrounded by gloom. Good memories become that voice of hope in times of despair that says to us that if life was once good, it could still be good again. Good memories become the silent whisper that says, *"This too shall pass"*. Nothing happens that is not supposed to happen.

Life is one great expression. Life seeks to express itself through us. All that human beings go through is part of life expressing itself. Sometimes, you may not agree with how life expresses itself through you, but it will do it anyway. Someone once said, *"Learn to let life be because, with or without your permission, life will still be"*. Anna Molnar also attests to this truth through the following statement; *"Whatever is going to happen, will happen whether we worry or not"*. In my philosophy class, I came across a Latin phrase, *"amor fati"*, which means loving your fate. When one loves his fate, he sees his suffering and loss as somehow necessary. We should have learned from being born without first being consulted that fate was always going to somehow find its way into our lives despite the availability of free will. Everything is balanced in this life, and the things you choose are equal to those that chose you.

Do not complain. Rather, appreciate the opportunity. Do not take offence; rather, appreciate the opportunity. What opportunity, you may ask? When hated, appreciate the opportunity to show unconditional love. When rejected, appreciate the opportunity to show unconditional acceptance. Do not suffer from, but get bliss from. When treated with contempt, appreciate the opportunity to show patience and tolerance. Learn to see opportunities for showing what is within you; prayers are not answered as expected. I appreciate opportunities to show Christ in you to the broken and bruised around you. Those who cause you to suffer are themselves in suffering; when we look at our offenders in this way, compassion and empathy flow genuinely from within to them. Those who are jealous, bitter and resentful towards you are the actual victims, not you. They are bound by chains beyond control. Any person who fights you is first at war with himself.

Violence cannot proceed from a peaceful person. The devil does not invent anything new, but he takes from what is already available within a person. The ego will seek to retaliate when you are to hold your peace, but with the help of the Holy Spirit, you can always be aided to be slow to anger. I have been in situations where I was tempted to fight back my way, but the Holy Spirit would remind me what the scripture says. I remember a time when a group of females had a negative attitude towards me where I stayed; my human nature wanted to retaliate. After all, it is what it is good at: eye for an eye, tooth for tooth. But that gentle voice from within me, which I know to be the Holy Spirit, reminded me to pray for those who ill-treat me, and when I obeyed, I found myself full of power to love my opponents and be patient with them. It then became clear to me that all that God commands is for my own good. He has His own way of saving us from harming ourselves.

"Pain is a gift. Everyone lives between the intervals of tears and joy. Every joy is an interval between two sorrows, and every sorrow is an interval between two joys. Compassion is simply entering another's pain."

– Muzi Cindi.

11 | Everything Is Burning

"There is no fixed reality, only endless possibilities.

What is here today may be gone tomorrow. What is intended for good may be tainted by evil. The friends you make today may turn out to be your greatest enemies tomorrow. Sometimes, you create your own enemies in the process of making friends. Although you may not be aware of it, your most trusted companions can be your greatest opponents. Be careful of what you utter and disclose in happy moments, for it can be turned into burning arrows against you in times of quarrel and conflict. You may be alive now, but in the blink of an eye, you could join the world of the dead. Danger and death always surround us; we walk with them, we sit with them, and when we sleep, they remain awake. They can occur in the depths of the night when a man is deep asleep.

Everything around one that one uses carries the potential to harm one. The car you use can injure and kill you, the knife in your kitchen can take away life, the pool outside your house can drown a person to death, the rope in your drawer can be used to take life and so forth. Every light casts a shadow, revealing that darkness exists alongside it. If a marriage of eighteen to thirty years can come to an end, what exactly is certain in this universe? In the Bible, Job was a wealthy man, but in the blink of an eye, without any warning, he turned into a peasant. One moment, he had everything, and in an instant, he lost it all. Life is one huge risk; we are always risking whether we are aware of it or not.

Nisha was on top of her career in 2018 as a model and a top actress in Indian movies. Companies competed to have her as their brand ambassador. In January 2019, she unfortunately got involved in an accident and was brought home to Nepal to wait for her death. One moment, everybody was attracted to her; another moment, everybody repelled her. That is life. Tread with caution and humility. The spiritual code of conduct says, "Just because something has never happened, don't assume it never will. And don't be deceived into believing that because something has always happened, it will continue".

What one considers an apple of one's eye could disappear in a blink of an eye. That is life, but we are living anyway because we are already here. Nonetheless, we have no guarantee on many things except for the moment we are currently in. Even some relationships and friendships are only seasonal in this life, and we sometimes hurt ourselves by treating them as permanent, which was meant to be seasonal. I have often seen people holding on to a relationship simply because they have been friends or together for a long time, even when the relationship is no longer helping them grow and evolve as individuals. We have to teach ourselves to lovingly detach from what no longer serves us. Lovingly detach, not bitterly. There is no need for hostility towards something simply because it no longer serves you; we can detach with love when we are enlightened enough to see that it is for our good and those around us.

There are tragic accidents that completely alter people's course of life unexpectedly; the person was fine one moment, but before they knew it, they are no longer able to walk; the list is endless of how people's lives changed in an instant when unexpected happened. Vincent van Gogh says, *"For my part, I know nothing with any certainty, but the sight of the stars makes me dream."* The only certainty he has is that which is found in the consistency of the stars. Nature has more certainty than human beings. The sun that has been rising in the east and setting in the west still does that to this day, so you can make any claim based on natural courses, and you can be certain of it because in nature, there we find certainty.

Everything is burning is a phrase highlighting uncertainty in and with everything in life. We might as well argue that to be attached to anything in this life is to be attached to uncertainty. Therefore, dive into the well of attachment fully informed so that when you bleed, you may bleed willingly and joyfully, knowing you have been warned of the pain of excessive attachment. Change is our sovereign governor; it occurs both for our advantage and disadvantage without making any announcement. Ironic as it may sound, uncertainty appears to be the most certain thing in this life. Everything is burning, like a flower that is here today and tomorrow gone, so are we. Teach yourself not to take everything too seriously; learn not to take everything too personally. Have some humorous approach towards life; after all, it is all vanity. Live and laugh, laugh and live.

Do not be in denial of uncertainty as an inevitable part of life because, after all, it is what it is. We did not choose things to be this way, but we must find a way to work with them for as long as we live. Existence comes with so many burdens; attachment is one of them. Losing the object of your attachment is not the exact direct cause of your pain, but attaching to the point of forgetting the impermanence of things is. Everything that exists is part of life, and uncertainty is no exception. When you make peace with the impermanence of things, uncertainty ceases to be a monster to you. When you are afraid of nothing, you are ready for anything.

You thought it would last forever, but it did not. You wish you could live forever, but you do not. Make peace with the endless possibilities of life because being too attached to the idea of a fixed reality only hurts you in the end. We exist within a cycle of endless possibilities; hence, there will always be unprecedented events occurring for as long as we live. Even if a person promises to love you forever, that does not mean they are always going to be there. Everything is in constant flux; the only true constant is change. Even who you are today may change tomorrow. The true masters of life are those who have learnt the importance of fluidity. Fluidity enhances our ability to adjust and adapt to the changes in life.

The Lord Jesus Christ says, *"The wind blows wherever it pleases"* I say, *"Life happens however it wants, even without your permission"*. There is a lot that we have to bear with as humanity, even though we do not approve of its occurrence. Life has no guarantee on many things. When you accept that anything is possible, you are immediately freed from the fear of what could go wrong. Life is a huge dare. It might go wrong, but I will dare try anyway. I might get hurt, but I will dare love anyway. It might not last, but I will dare try anyway. You might not find but dare seek it anyway. When you open up to all the possibilities, you open up to all that life has to offer, both pleasurable and painful. There is a pain that is necessary to feel, and that is the pain of trying and failing, the pain of longing for permanence in a world of impermanence, and the pain of seeking and not finding. Impermanence and uncertainty govern us, but dare anyway. It is better to dare, no matter the outcome, than not to dare at all.

When we say, '*This too shall pass,*' we should bear in mind that this statement is applicable not only to difficult moments but also to good and pleasurable moments- they too, do pass. My mortality reminds me that nothing lasts forever in this world. My view of death is not one of death as a monster but a form of rest that one does need at a certain point of their lives after all that life has put them through. Immortality is a blessing to be enjoyed in a state of paradise; in such a world, it could only be torture. The course in miracles says, "One day, you will realize that death is not the punishment but the reward. And it says that birth is not the beginning of life but a continuation. And physical death is not the end of life but a continuation". According to Lao Tzu, life is a series of natural and spontaneous changes and resisting these changes only creates sorrow. He says let reality be reality. Let things flow naturally forward in whatever way they like.

"Thanks to impermanence, anything is possible."

– Thich Nhat Hanh

12 | Heal It Or Relive It

We are bound to relive whatever we do not heal from. Pain has the power to recreate pain in such a way that the life of a person can become an endless pain. I have heard many stories of different individuals who experienced the same ordeal in different stages of their lives, the most common of which is that of rape. I was watching a certain American show aimed at bringing holistic healing to families. A mother of four children came with her daughters and told Iyanla Vanzant that she was raped as a child and nobody in her family, not even her children, knew about it.

Surprisingly, her three daughters had also been raped, but she did not know about it. This taught me the danger of procreating without first healing ourselves as individuals. If we are a wounded generation, we will give birth to wounded offspring. Hidden pains and unhealed traumas are hereditary. Just because you kept something hidden from your family, children or friends to the extent of dying with it doesn't mean it is hidden from your genes. What is hidden from the eyes and ears of people is not necessarily hidden from our genes. If you hide something, you must also secretly seek professional help to help you heal from it.

Pain feeds on pain, as they say, so if you have locked in pain within yourself, you are most likely to experience more and more pain in different stages of your life. It is said of a dog bite that if one can be bitten by a dog, other dogs can smell it when one passes. The same is true of untreated emotional pain; it keeps attracting more and more pain. Of traumatic events, it is said that if you have not healed from it, each time you think about it, your body produces the exact same chemicals as when it happened. That means you relive the experience hundreds of times simply because you have not let it go.

As a counsellor, I noticed that most of the time, when people have been through something traumatic and painful, the most common response is that of wanting to forget about it. Forgetting and healing are not the same; in fact, there is no such thing as intentional forgetting; hence, the more you want to forget, the more you remember. You do not heal by forgetting because your behaviour is not affected only by what you are conscious of; even that which you are unconscious of still affects you. It is not only the mind that remembers; even the body does. You do not need to think about what you were doing during the day to feel tired, but as you sit at night on your couch, the body brings it all back.

What, then, could be a solution to breaking completely from being haunted by past pains? Steve Aitchison says, *"Emotional pain is not something that should be hidden away and never spoken about. There is truth in your pain, there is growth in your pain, but only if it is first brought out into the open"*. To concord with Aitchison, Adyashanti says, *"Everything you blame, you are stuck with. Bless it. Wish it well.*

I wish it its own freedom, and it will be very powerful in that it will not come back to you. If you do not forgive it, if you do not bless it, if you do not wish it well, the energy will just be magnetically drawn back to you because it is looking for resolution. All negative energy that we have inherited is there because it is looking for a resolution.

What happened to you may not be your fault, but healing from it definitely is your responsibility. Some of the emotional wounds we carry are incurred as a result of not knowing better and, therefore, not being able to do better. As a human being, at any given point and under any given circumstance, you always try to do your best with the information, knowledge, understanding and resources available to you. You asked people for permission to be who you know you were meant to be, and they did not understand you, so forgive yourself.

You expect people to do exactly what you would do given the same situation, but they do not because they are not you. For that, also forgive yourself. You blamed and judged because you never gave yourself time to understand where people were coming from and for them to behave the way they did. For that, you also forgive yourself. You criticized and ridiculed what you did not understand, only to find yourself doing exactly that afterwards; it is part of being human; it happens. Forgive and let go. Forgiveness is part of healing, and it should not be forced but genuine. David Augsburger tells us, "When forgiveness denies that there is anger, acts as if it is all forgotten- do not offer it, do not trust it, do not depend on it. It is not forgiveness; it is a magical fantasy". Sometimes, we forgive the other, but the more enlightened we become, we realize that it is ourselves we have to forgive the most.

Forgive yourself for having trusted people too much, for it was that too much trust that resulted in being hurt so much when it was broken. It is convenient and comforting to our fragile selves to keep blaming, but it really doesn't help us much to keep blaming. Rather, we remain stuck with what we are blaming. May we be given the grace we need not to allow our egos to hinder our healing, I pray. Malena Crawford tells us that each time you forgive another and release the beliefs that you created around your memories, you are healing your wounds and sealing the door to your inner peace. Each time we keep our eyes fixed on the loss, it becomes difficult for us to forgive. If you see the partner who cheated on you as having wasted your time as opposed to having given you lessons for what to be careful of next time, you will be imprisoned by unforgiveness. I learned from a certain man that in this life, you have neither enemies nor friends; you only have teachers. Every person in your life serves a specific purpose that will help you to evolve and rise to who you were destined to be.

We heal when we take full charge of our healing; that means becoming aware that your healing is dependent on your attitude and response towards your hurt and not necessarily who or what bruised you. "Who" may not apologize. "What" may not give you the answers you seek, but you can take full charge and transform. We sometimes, without realizing it, develop an attachment to our brokenness, which makes our healing seem very difficult even when it is not that difficult. I remember back in the days as a child, how I enjoyed the special treatment I got due to being sick to the point that being sick ended up not being so bad because it afforded me the attention I do not normally get. George Bernard Shaw once stated, "People become too attached to their burdens sometimes more than the burdens are attached to them".

Hence, it does not surprise me when people become too attached to their brokenness because of the pity and attention they are getting. A certain level of pity is not good for our healing process; it can keep us in the same place for a long time. There must be a willingness to heal. Everything in this universe works with us only when we are willing to work with it. Healing requires us to open up to it and be intentional about our healing processes. The power and importance of intentionality when it comes to healing cannot be left unmentioned because the lack of intention inhibits one from taking the necessary action crucial for one's healing.

Dale Carnegie, in his book, states, 'Man, it is not pity you need but a push'. We should know when to offer pity and when to give a push towards healing and transformation. When Jesus Christ came to the man by the pool of Bethesda who had been lame for thirty-eight years, His question to him was, "Do you want to be made well?" As people, we tend to make the mistake of assuming that every broken person wants to be made well, and sometimes it is not the case. There should be wisdom to see when an individual has become too attached to their brokenness because the best way in such situations is first to help them detach from the normalized abnormal so that they can proceed towards emotional healing and wholeness. A fresh and different perspective on a matter is always vital in helping the person see that there is life beyond the reality to which they have succumbed.

In the Bible, in the book of Acts 5:15-16, we find people bringing the sick and those tormented by unclean spirits that the shadow of Peter might fall on them and those on whom it fell found healing. The dark shadows you are hiding, blaming and ashamed of could be a remedy for someone. The past experiences and mistakes you are busy blaming could be the shadow that someone out there needs to know that they are not the first to go through whatever they are going through. Your dark shadows have healing for someone out there. You could be hiding the very thing that God intends to use.

After you have bled, have the courage to wear your scars with pride like Jesus Christ, who was not ashamed of his scars. Healing comes with the embrace of our shadow. The acceptance of where we have been and what we have been through. You cease to be a prisoner of where you have been and what you have been through when you are no longer ashamed of it. Jesus Christ, after his resurrection from death, had scars and piercings of where He had been, but He was not bound to nor by where He had been. Memories and scars of what you have been through should not become an identity. Let us not turn occurrences into personal identities.

God can create an ointment for others out of your ailments. In psychology, we have what we call post-traumatic growth, which is a stage wherein the one who suffered trauma is now able to make meaning of the traumatic event and is no longer a victim of it. We should grow through what we go through so that we are not affected tomorrow by what affects us today as though we have never encountered it in our lives. You will know you have reached the final stage of healing when you are using what happened to you to help others. Healing is painful, but the feeling of being healed is priceless.

According to Jeff Foster, healing, for the most part, means grieving. You won't get through something without grieving. Disappointment is sacred. You have to grieve out the past, the things you lost, the roads you could have taken. You have to grieve your stolen childhood, those shattered dreams, a life you thought you were meant to live. You have to grieve out those missed opportunities, words and behaviours you regret, choices, made or unmade, that led you to where you are or not.

You have to grieve out the dream that it could have been any different, the lie that you believed in order to keep yourself going, or keep yourself safe, or keep you on the pathless path to where you find yourself now. Let yourself be disappointed, then! Turn towards the pain of "things not turning out the way I wanted them to'. This is the death of your ego, and it hurts like hell sometimes.

"God cannot heal what you refuse to reveal. One day, you will have to tell your story of how you overcame what you went through, and it will be someone else's survival guide. Do not hide your scars."

– Kina Dolphin

13 | Finding Closure Heals Us

My experience as a counsellor taught me that some people are distressed because they do not understand. They do not understand why what happened to them had to happen to them; they do not understand why they do what they do at times the way they do it. They do not understand why life must be the way it is for them. They do not understand why God must do things the way He does them. They are confused by why the world is as it is. I once had to normalize a situation for a client, and she never came back for a follow-up session because, to her, it was confusing how she had acted under a certain circumstance that I will not disclose here, and after having validated her response, she found peace with how she had acted. This experience made me realize that, sometimes, the cause of people's distress is confusion about an event, not necessarily the event itself. When people gain a deeper and clearer understanding of something they went through or why they behaved the way they did in a situation, it puts them at ease with themselves and the situation. It is possible to go through an experience without understanding its meaning, and as soon as you grasp the meaning behind the experience, you find healing in it. The 'whys' after an occurrence are a sign of a meaning that was missed by the one who went through the experience.

The mind always seeks to make sense of life and its events; if it cannot, existential suffering—described by philosophers—can set in. You begin to suffer because of your very existence. You want to know and understand why you are here, but you just don't; you want to understand why people suffer and why there must be a thing as tragic and painful as death. You begin to question until the questions become the cause of your distress and misery In his book *Man's Search for Meaning*, Victor E. Frankl states, "It is normal to behave abnormally under abnormal circumstances."

At times, this is all that people need to hear to be able to heal from guilt and regrets and move on with their lives. Sometimes, people act instinctively in ambiguous situations to protect themselves, and later, when things calm down, they begin to question their actions. If they cannot find answers, distress might set in. Understanding is a prerequisite for acceptance. You cannot fully accept what you cannot clearly understand, but at times, even the ability to let go of the need to understand is necessary.

Many people are emotionally and spiritually ill because of not understanding, and not understanding breeds resistance instead of acceptance. An abandoned child wants to know and understand why he or she was abandoned. A dumped girlfriend wants to understand why she had to be dumped after having tried her level best to be the best partner to her boyfriend. A person with a calling wants to know why it had to be him or her out of so many people, and from personal experience, I can relate here to a certain degree. When you are called, there are times when you may question your calling with the aim of setting yourself free from it. There are times you think that it could all be just in your mind, but sadly, it is not. I have been there. Life throws us punches that leave us seeking closure from time to time, but from personal experience, I have learned that if you remain connected to the Holy Spirit, He has a unique way of connecting even the most confusing dots of one's life so that you find the closure you most seek.

There were times when I wished churches did not exist just so that I could be free from the chains of destiny. You see churches being established, rising and falling, and you wonder why God allowed what He has called a person to fall. You see pastors going through so much, and you wonder if it is all worth it. You see a man suffering health problems because of ministry, and you wonder why. You see a person suffering because of the very people he left everything for, and you wonder if it was all worth it. We all have our fair share of *"whys"*, and I am no exception. I have had my *"whys"*. Sometimes, these questions evolve into deeper ones *"Where is God?"* It was only later on when I noticed that my perception and understanding of God were undergoing transformation, that my *"whys"* were resolved.

Pain and suffering can alter one's relationship with God. There is no awakening or enlightenment without its own costs. There is a price to be paid to access certain levels and dimensions of God. In the Garden of Eden, after they had eaten the fruit, the Bible says their eyes were opened, and they gained knowledge of good and evil. But they lost the garden. They gained enlightenment but lost Eden. There was a loss and gain situation. There is a price for accessing certain depths of God; some insights and revelations will not come through studying the Word, but they will require experiential learning on your part. But God is faithful; He will ensure that you live to tell the tale to others.

One of the wounds that still need to be dealt with is what one fellow of mine calls the "God-wound". This is the wound that has left us with many deep scars. The wound that left us asking ourselves why our prayers were not answered, yet we were told prayer solves all problems. The wound that emerges because God did not come through for your dying beloved family member. Although this wound appears to be directly linked to God, it is, in actual fact, a result of what we are taught about God. It was Marie Satori who said that in your journey, there will be "in-between times" of transition. You may feel lost, confused, angry, unseen, or empty. Do not confuse these times of transition as a forever state of being or broken. You are breaking away from what was, creating space for what will be.

God is invisible, so how one relates with Him is based on what one was taught about Him. It is more a matter of what you were told about Him, not necessarily Him. For instance, if a person says, "Why is the world in such suffering if God is truly compassionate?" This statement, though it sounds like questioning God, is more based on what a person knows or was taught about God. It is easier for someone who is told about a God who does not allow us to suffer peril to question Him when peril strikes than someone who is told that they will still face suffering in this life despite walking with God.

When faith does not materialize, it leaves a deep wound; we need to admit that for us to find closure and heal. I want to speak as a human being here who can relate to the frustrations of other human beings and say you do have the right to question God sometimes, and you are going to be angry with Him at times. But God cannot help you if you are angry from within; neither can you have the peace of God if you are not at peace with God. As a counsellor, one of the problems I have picked up is that when Christians feel that they have been somehow disappointed by God for not meeting them at their point of need, it is hard for them to come clean and open about it.

They would rather talk in circles instead of expressing exactly what is going on in their hearts and minds. If you hide, you cannot be helped. In so saying, I am not trivializing the reality of shame we feel as human beings when having to share our problems. It happens to most of us. There are things that are not easy to talk about, especially those involving shame, pain, guilt and regret. Pain knows the power of expression; hence, it makes it difficult for us to talk about it because we begin to heal from it when we cough it out of our chest. Emotional pain sustains itself through shame and guilt.

Anyone who goes through a tragedy of some sort wants to understand why. You may think people need so much for them to heal when, in fact, they just need to understand. Understanding is the cure for confusing calamities. Not knowing can be painful; not understanding is even worse. Martha Mkhize says that she only started sharing her life story when she began understanding her life purpose. I can personally relate to this; when your life purpose becomes clear, and you realize that what you thought were thorns were actually crowns, shame disappears.

I never spent a lot of time with my mother as she would be away due to work, although I was very much a momma's boy compared to my twin brother. We were like Jacob and Esau; one enjoyed being indoors, and the other enjoyed being outdoors. Like most South African youth, my father was not there, but he had done his best by being an instrument of destiny and bringing me to this world. At first, I was somewhat resentful of his absence, but when I fully awakened to my life purpose, I realized that it all happened exactly the way it was meant to. My mother passed away in 2003 while we were staying with my aunt in Ladysmith. We were then raised by my uncle, but trust me when I say I am grateful for every moment of it. We do not orchestrate our destinies, but when we flow in harmony with them, everything makes sense, and even the seemingly unforgivable becomes forgivable. When you finally realize that you had to be here, how you came into this world and how you grew up becomes a tiny matter. You are here now, and that is what matters the most. You had to be here at all costs.

Understanding is supreme. In the Bible, Apostle Paul was made to understand the reason behind the thorn in his flesh. Sometimes, we do not need the removal of certain things we are uncomfortable with, but a mere understanding of why they are there, at times, is sufficient. Understanding the 'why' could mark the beginning of the most needed shift from pain to purpose. There are times when you may not find answers to your 'why', should such happen to you, shift from asking why it happened and ask 'what did it teach you instead'.

As you grow, you will also start understanding that, under certain circumstances, giving up the need to know is another aspect of spiritual maturity. I have prayed hurt, I have prayed discouraged, I have prayed confused, I have prayed frustrated, I have prayed to doubt, and I have prayed uncertain—why was I praying though, in these conditions, I do not know; nonetheless, I prayed. I did not understand why I continued praying even though what I had prayed for did not happen, but guess what? I prayed anyway.

What makes the waiting most difficult for us as human beings, is not knowing when the awaited will arrive. It is not knowing when prayers will be answered that makes people impatient and eventually give up praying. I still recall how impatient I would become when my publishers were quiet, not saying anything to me; I would need a word from them to silence my impatience because not being updated on how everything was going bothered me so much.

A fellow classmate at tertiary once shared a story with me of a doctor whose brother was killed in a failed car hijacking. It is said that during the trial, the offender explained why he had been part of the hijacking; he explained that he came from a poverty-stricken family and both his parents are HIV positive. The doctors made efforts to validate his statement and found that everything he said was true. Something unexpected happened because of understanding where the offender was coming from; instead of asking for a harsher sentence, the doctors whose brother had been killed offered to care for the offender's sick parents took care of his siblings and visited him during his imprisonment.

Understanding the 'why' shed light and resulted in a reaction you wouldn't normally expect from someone whose brother had been killed. Even as human beings, we are drawn to spaces where we feel understood; we are attracted to those who show an understanding of us. We are not asking for much, just to be understood. Being understood not only validates our existence but also heals us as it enables us to find closure about the most hard-to-understand parts of ourselves and our world.

In the Old Testament (2 Samuel, 12:15-22), we learn of King David, who had a sick child. The Bible says while the child was sick, David neither stood from the floor nor did he eat anything. But when the child died, he got up from the ground, washed, put on lotions, changed his clothes and went to the house of the Lord to worship. While the child was still alive, there was hope, but when it died, he had to accept what it was. Death brought him closure on the situation that it could not be salvaged. When we accept what is, we find the strength to get up from the ground of pain and misery to continue with life. Accept and get up. Accept and heal. Accept and move on.

"Whoever is patient has great understanding, but one who is quick-tempered displays folly."

– Proverbs 14:29.

14 | Empty Yourself and Free Yourself

Emptying oneself is the greatest form of wisdom. Emptying ourselves offers us the greatest form of relief from suffering, pain, and anguish. We suffer greatly because of all that we have filled ourselves with. As human beings, we are always taking in things from the world around us through our senses: our sense of hearing, our sense of touch, our sense of taste, and our sense of smell, but mostly through our sense of sight. We are loaded with endless cravings and desires because of our senses. We hear and wish, we see and desire, but when we suffer because of what we have accumulated because of our senses, we forget to empty ourselves. Humanity is always in search of something, in pursuit of something, in need of something, in want of this, in desire of that all because of the senses that are always collecting information for us from the outside physical world. We were never taught to empty ourselves when needed to regain our peace, balance, and sanity.

Right now, you are most probably unhappy, feeling miserable and incomplete because of something you saw and wished to have but are unable to attain. You hoped too much, dreamed too much, and expected too much, and now all of it is hurting you deeply. You do not always need to get what you want to be happy; sometimes, what you truly need is to release the desires or wishes that have entered through your senses. I am of the view that if we can fill ourselves through our senses, we can also most definitely empty ourselves when that which we have filled ourselves with is causing us nothing but pain and misery. You have power over the attachment to your desires and wishes, to free yourself from them if their unfulfillment seems to be causing you a lot of pain. It is good to pursue, but it is wrong to put your happiness in the hands of what you are in pursuit of because even after finding it, you might still find that you are not happy.

Your senses have filled you with so much, and now you feel so incomplete because of what the senses have filled you with. We were never taught to take time to empty ourselves at times that is why humanity is burdened by so much. If we had been taught to empty ourselves when necessary to do so, we would not struggle to let go of what needs to be released. Consciously and unconsciously, we create our own suffering through the attachments we form to things that enter our hearts through our senses, and when we suffer, we forget that we can reclaim our freedom, inner peace and joy through offloading and detaching. There are many things you desire and crave that you saw somewhere, which I believe you would not be desiring and craving if you did not have sight.

You have role models in whose footsteps you would love to follow. You have dream cars that you would love to see yourself driving one day. There is that latest phone that has become your obsession, but where did it all begin? It began when you saw with your eyes and heard with your ears. Had you neither seen nor heard, I doubt you would be so bothered by the absence of these things in your life. We are unconscious slaves and prisoners of our own senses. But right here and now, you are being invited to take that step of reevaluating your life, your dreams, your goals, and your desires, emptying yourself of certain things and regaining your inner peace and joy while allowing life to be life independent of your expectations of it.

You have accumulated so many wishes, desires and cravings that have enslaved you and reduced you to living and valuing nothing else other than money. You are unhappy now because of the countless cravings your senses have brought you. You are dissatisfied with your life because the cravings you have developed, nurtured, and harboured in you have made you think that you need a lot of money to be happy. Just a friendly reminder: there was a time when you did not have much money, and you could still be happy; how did it happen then? How did you do it then? If you could do it then, you can most certainly do it now. As a child, you did not have much money, but you were very happy; you found joy in the simplest of things. Everything revolved in the now; there were no worries about the future, no feelings of inadequacy due to lacking a certain status.

You enjoyed life for being alive. You were just happy to be; you were happy to be alive; you were happy to be aware, and you were happy to be you until life loaded you with so much that you had to strive to attain to feel complete and happy. But right here and now, I ask you to allow me to take you back to the former, happier and fulfilled you. You do not need much but just yourself and God if you do believe. I am calling you to unconditional gratitude, which is the simplest form of abundance. I am calling you to say yes fully to life right where you are.

I am calling you who has been disappointed a lot; I am calling you who has been chasing without reaching; I am calling you who has been aiming without catching. It is not by mistake, nor is it a coincidence, for this book to be in your hands at this moment; gratitude, the power that makes all things enough, is calling you out of your misery. Jon Kabat-Zinn encourages us to connect with the ground of this moment and embrace our life with its "ten thousand joys and ten thousand sorrows". He describes this as the "ultimate love affair" – a love affair with life on its own terms.

I am shifting your eyes and focus from the destination, and I am bringing them into the journey itself. I am saying to you, enjoy yourself right where you are; do not wait to reach somewhere before you can be happy. Do not postpone your joy and happiness for a goal whose time to be achieved you do not know. Do not deprive yourself of all that the journey has for you for the destination. Do not miss out on the bliss of the trial because of the awaited triumph. Right where you are, I am convinced that you have all that you could possibly need to be happy.

Just as you can think about all that makes you feel incomplete and sad, you can also think about all that makes life worth living. It is all there within you. We have placed our happiness in the hands of many things except ourselves. We can never be in charge of our happiness for as long as it depends on things and other people. We should learn to fully own our joy and that means realising that you, yourself and you are responsible for it – not others or things.

Realising that people are responsible for their own happiness will also set you free from the need and burden to always make others happy. A lot of us suffered immensely as a result of the 'people-pleasing syndrome' because we did not know that people were responsible for their own happiness. I am not against making others happy; there is nothing wrong with that, provided it is not at the expense of your own happiness, authenticity and values. I do a lot of humanitarian work, and I cannot begin to describe the feeling it gives me to see smiles on people's faces because of what I did for them. I make them happy but not in a way that violates my authentic self, and I believe that is how it should be.

Empty yourself of complaints and fill your mind and heart with gratitude. Empty yourself of the dissatisfactions and find satisfaction with life. Empty yourself into thinking that you must reach somewhere to be happy and start appreciating the present moment for what it is. Empty yourself into thinking that you must acquire something to be someone; by virtue of being, you are already someone of worth. You have human rights that protect you and your dignity as a human being despite your class, social or financial status, whether you are disabled or able; by virtue of being human, you have human rights because you are as valuable as that independent of what you have or may not have.

Nothing in the future is going to make you happy if you fail to be happy where you are. Your joy awaits your realisation of what you already have right in this present moment, not in the distant future. On social media, I once came across a very interesting quote: *"Beware of destination addiction, the idea that happiness is in the next place, the next job, or even with the next partner. Until you give up the idea that happiness is somewhere else, it will never be where you are.*

In his movie entitled *"Fearless"*, Jet Li became very *obsessed with fame and status. He did not care much about anything except to be the champion; to him, life was all about winning and having masses cheering for you. As a result, he lost the people closest and dearest to him due to his obsession with fame and status. At one time, he took his friend to the battle ring where they normally compete in a physical fight and told his friend about the places he was left with so he could become the regional champion. At that, the friend responded by saying, "But you would still be you after having won all those fights". None of his friend's words made much sense to him then until he reached a point in his life where he hit rock bottom when his mother and daughter were killed, and he started realising his mistakes and how much he had neglected his real treasure because of obsession with fame and status, in the process of being too attached to something, he neglected what mattered the most.*

When his friend said to him, *'You would still be you after having won those fights'*, I believe he was trying to show him the vanity and superficiality of his obsession. May we not become too attached to what is passing and superficial and end up chasing and acquiring it at the expense of what matters the most. Though what you have can be taken away from you, you can never be stripped of who you are. Give value where value is really due.

Empty yourself and be free. Empty yourself of the need for external validation and approval; you never needed those while in your mother's womb. Empty yourself of the need to want everything to go your way; you are not the one who set the period you stayed in your mother's womb; nonetheless, you complied. Empty yourself of the need to have your offenders apologise before you can forgive; your healing process will always be dependent on someone else other than you if you do that. *Najwa Zebian* asks, "Do you really need to have someone telling you how they have hurt you when you yourself know very well how it felt? It may be a want, but is it really a need for that person to tell you how you were hurt because you yourself felt that pain? They may do it, but do you really need it? It may be good to get it, but is it a need?" Her words challenge us to empty ourselves of the need for an apology before we can heal and move on but to learn to move on even without it. Acknowledge your hurt and the intensity of its pain, but by no means give someone the power to determine the 'when' of your healing. I have been forgiving a lot of people who did not apologise. It is a doable thing when you live a life based on who you are, not who they are.

Being able to surrender is a strength on its own. Do not be afraid nor hesitant to surrender. You could be carrying a mountain that you are meant to climb. You could be resisting what you are supposed to allow yourself to feel. You could be resisting a moment that has come to teach you something. Surrender. Learn to surrender to the moment when it is necessary to do so. I learnt to surrender to the moment at a certain point in my life, and it gave me relief from the pressures I had placed myself under.

Learn to surrender to time, for it is, after all, the master of us all. I also learnt to surrender to times when things did not happen at a time in which I wanted them to happen. I learnt the power of surrender, and it saved me from many sorrows. Sometimes, suffering is a result of resisting what you are supposed to be surrendering to. Some state of affairs will not change; you will be the one to change. When you surrender where surrendering is necessary, you prove to yourself and the world that you are wise enough to see and accept when something is beyond your control. You show that you are mature and humble enough to work not against but with your human limitations.

"In the spiritual life, one becomes just like a little child- without resentment, without attachment, full of life and joy."
– Paramahansa Yogananda

15 | Apology from Life to Humanity

You came to me not of your own choosing, and you had to find a manual for bearing with me because I never gave you any. For that, I am very sorry. You were left with no other choice but to create a manual for yourself by yourself. I, Life, sincerely and profusely apologise for having put you through such a difficult time. I wanted to be your best experience, but I have somehow turned into your greatest nightmare. The goal was to be an experience for you to have and be happy, but somehow, I have become a problem to be solved for some members of the family of humanity.

I am aware, I acknowledge, and I apologise. You have done so many things in so many ways to try and master me, but each time, I just prove myself to be an unsolvable riddle. With all your wisdom, curiosity and understanding, you have not fully figured me out. Even those who at once thought they had it all under control, walked with boastfulness, looked with conceit, and reacted with arrogance were brought low by me. I have proven to so many that none can master me unless they master themselves. I am sorry that your lack of insight and understanding kept you trying to master me for so many years when you could have made things easier for yourselves by mastering yourselves.

I am in a predicament you did not choose. I am a war you did not choose. You were only given a limited choice of weapons through which you could fight for yourselves and stand your ground. Your swings and oscillations between victory and defeat, success and failure bear testimony to how limited the weapons you have for the battle of life, my battle. From time to time, you are visited by uncertainty, confronted by adversity, and overtaken by tragedy. Oh, dear human, I am aware of it all, and I admit that it is harm you incurred by coming into existence that you would not have known or experienced had you not come into existence. According to Christians, I was ruined and corrupted by Adam and Eve's eating of the forbidden fruit. According to Buddhists, I am suffering whose root cause is craving, and to eliminate me as suffering, you should get rid of the desire.

Friedrich Nietzsche also theorised of me as suffering, and surviving me as suffering requires finding meaning in me despite the appalling and disastrous occurrences of my life. There is a lot that you had to bear with because of me, and for that, I greatly and deeply commend you. I am life. You are living with me daily, but you hardly have time to engage with me. At times, I disrupt your normal routines and deter your tours in the hope that I will get your attention and you will get the bounty messages and lessons I have for you. I come through tragic experiences to shake you out of your security and remind you of the impermanence of things that you so long and cry for day and night.

Half of the time, you do not even know what you are doing. You sometimes create problems while trying to solve problems. You try your best, but your best just does not seem to be enough for me because I am teaching you that your best must be enough for you, not me. But because I never told you beforehand, I sincerely apologise. For the mistakes you have made, I offer my forgiveness, which you did not ask for; please forgive yourself, too. You need not ask for my forgiveness; I fully own up to what I have put you through, dear human. I have touched you more than I can count with the heavy hands of suffering, pain and sorrow; the intention was to open your inner eyes and give you insight because I know that sight alone is not enough. You only see the visible with sight, but insight is needed for the invisible. I wanted you to see the unseen so that you can do the undone. Once again, I apologise for the confusion it caused you that kept you wondering, 'Why you?'

By now, you should at least be aware that I delight in remaining an unsolvable riddle and take pleasure in being a hidden mystery that leaves humanity with the duty of explaining and interpreting. I am sorry for it all; I apologise for life for all that humanity must go through. Trying to understand me, not to mention trying to understand what happens to you when I depart from you, and you cease to live. Not only are you bothered by questions of existence but, even worse, those of your nonexistence, too. Being alive makes you think, 'Why live?'

and dying makes you wonder, 'Where am I going?' You have so much to deal with humans, and I am fully aware.

You have desires that you did not choose, even though you are said to be a free agent who acts out of free will. I would love to argue that, in fact, you have never been free. You are just not aware of the chains that bind you. At times, you are provoked into jealousy, although you do not want to. In your mind, you have thoughts you wish you could silence, but you cannot; it was not in your power whether to acquire them or not. Nonetheless, they came. Your war is both within and without, which makes me wonder if there really is a hell waiting for you after existence has subjected you to so much torture. You have experienced so much of hell here despite your countless efforts to create a heaven for yourself. I am struggling to believe that there could still be another torture waiting for you after we part our separate ways. All that you deserve after we have parted our different ways is a peaceful rest where you can no longer remember the pangs of having been alive.

In consideration of your burden, I have a plea, an earnest request, an appeal of goodwill; please be kind and compassionate to yourself. I am not asking you much, but you show a little compassion and kindness to yourself. I am sorry for allowing you for the longest time to be so hard on yourself, but I am at this moment, as an offender, fully aware of his offences, admitting my impediments to you and therefore asking you to forgive yourself because I have forgiven you for doing what seemed best to you at that moment in time with the knowledge you had. Have mercy on yourself and other human beings like you. Your brothers and sisters are also fighting their own demons some of which you may know and others which you do not know.

Many have labelled me as rough, hard, and unfair, but in truth, I am just what you human beings make me be. Some of you were so overwhelmed by me that you consequently decided to take me from yourselves and ceased to be amongst the living. I wish there was more I could do to lessen your burden, but my apology, sympathy and empathy is the best I can offer. Some of you are subjected to hard and harsh realities that force you to find solace, even in fantasies that can never become a reality. You have resorted to making the house of mourning your home since the laughter of feasting is short-lived.

I do commend you, though. For finding me precious despite it all. For valuing me above gold. For approaching me with unconditional gratitude. I have peeked through hospital windows where I saw women bowing by your side in prayer to ensure I do not depart from you. I saw your bank notification of the millions withdrawn to preserve your life. I saw your willingness to pay whatever amount of money that was needed for your protection after having been threatened with death. I saw your fear and avoidance of cars after that tragic accident that nearly separated us.

I closely listened during your recuperation period as you told your friends how you nearly lost your life, and you now know what matters the most in me: life. I stand in constant awe of your continuous and unceasing appreciation of me despite all that you went through because of me. I want you to be constantly aware of the greatest gift you have been given in your suffering, the assured presence of the Divine One who is inseparable from you. The greatest gift you have been given in your suffering is the gift of the divine presence of the Almighty. In the perpetual suffering, there is also a perpetual gift of the presence for your strengthening.

I AM LIFE, AND THIS IS MY APOLOGY FOR YOUR SCARS AND TRAGEDIES, ACCOMPANIED BY MY APPRECIATION OF YOUR UNCONDITIONAL LOVE FOR ME AND YOUR UNCONDITIONAL GRATITUDE TOWARDS ME. I HONOUR YOUR RESILIENCE THROUGH AND DESPITE IT ALL.
YOU ARE STRONG AND RESILIENT, OH HUMAN!

16 | Prayer for Emotional Healing

"I pray that the God of all comfort would meet you amid your pain. That those around you will be patient as you process.

I pray that you will make space for the waves of intense emotion and you will remember to breathe. Every feeling has a voice, has a story, and every one of them, our God understands.

Breathe in the bitter ache as you sit through memories now stained in pain and exhale. You are loved. You are not alone. Your feelings deserve a seat at this table.

I pray life will become sweet again. That each step will gradually lessen in its weight and joy will find you again."

Amen.

– The Jasmine Sims

Prayer for One Struggling to Forgive

I pray that you will be able to see your offenders as God saw Nineveh. I pray that in place of judgment, mercy will take over. Like Joseph in Egypt, I pray that God opens your eyes for you to see that your perpetrators were actually the victims of your purpose. I pray that your eyes become open for you to see that what people planned for evil against you, God meant it for good. I pray that you see the connection in the different events of your life.

I pray that your eyes become open so that you can see that some of the people who left you had to leave you; it was not up to them, but it was at the hands of destiny. I pray that you realise that even if they wanted to stay, they would have not been able to. I pray that you realise that some of what happened to you had a lot to do with you and your purpose than the people who did it to you. I pray that you realise that your destiny had requirements that were very costly, which you were not aware of; I pray you realise that some of the people you think owe you an apology, but it is actually you who owe it to them.

I pray for you to find healing from that abandonment, rejection and hurt that is holding your life back. I pray for you to understand that even if your father would have loved to raise you, he wouldn't have been able to. I pray for you to realise that even if your mother wanted to be there for you, she wouldn't have been able to. I pray for you to understand and accept that your trials served the purpose of awakening and transforming you, not killing you.

May you receive a fresh and divine perspective on all that happened to you and the grace to let go of all the harboured grudges? May you be given the grace you need to forgive what you need to forgive and put behind you what needs to be left behind. I pray that you will start to see human beings and all that they have put you through as God sees it. I pray that, like Jesus Christ, you will operate at a level of understanding that it all happened according to God's purpose and intercede for their forgiveness. I pray that you will have your 'whys' answered, your confusions clarified, and realise that it all happened exactly the way it was supposed to. I pray you understand that forgiveness has more to do with you and your peace than the person who offended you.

I pray for you to come to an understanding that if their reality was your reality, their background your background, their experiences your experiences, their pain your pain and their understanding your understanding, you would have most probably acted like them. I pray you become aware that everybody is right according to their level of consciousness and understanding and that you cannot force people to understand what they are not yet ready to understand. I pray you come to an awareness that human beings hardly understand what they are doing, although they appear to be certain of their doings.

I pray you become transparent with God and acknowledge that by nature, you are vengeful, desiring an eye for an eye and tooth for a tooth, but through His help, you can be forgiving. I pray for your divinity to supersede your humanity, where your humanity says, hold the grudge and don't let it go. May your divinity emerge with grace and enable you to forgive, for it is indeed human to desire vengeance, but it is divine to forgive. The divinity of your soul is embedded in the ability to forgive. Though you may not forget, I pray for you to be given the grace to forgive.

17 | Prayer for Deep Seated Traumas

I pray that the God who sees where you cannot see may reach for you where you cannot reach for yourself. I pray for your innermost being, where all your life experiences accumulate and subconsciously affect your behaviour; I pray for the broken parts of your being affecting you without your knowledge and awareness; I declare the Lord's divine healing upon them. Through the immeasurable power of the Almighty, may there be a divine intervention in those parts of yourself that have found comfort in brokenness? All the causes unknown to you that are nonetheless affecting you, may they come to the surface.

I pray for your courage to attend therapy and face what you are avoiding. I pray for strength for you to confront your brokenness. I pray you do not bleed on people who did not cut you. I pray God will give you the wisdom to locate what needs to be located. I pray you find the help you need and be free from the flashbacks and nightmares of what you went through. I pray that you find enlightenment to understand what is happening to you and what to do with it.

May all the unconscious trauma residue in your system become conscious and stop controlling your life as though it is fate. May all the traumatic experiences of the past that have created phobias in you lose their hold over you.

May you find the strength and courage to allow yourself to fully feel the pain that keeps rearing its head, demanding to be felt by you. May all the avenues designed and wired for self-healing in your body be active as you allow yourself to face what you have been hiding from? I pray you will not brush off thoughts related to the traumatic experiences when they visit, but you will have the wisdom to observe them without judgment and receive the message they are bringing. I pray you will pay attention to your triggers and what they are telling you about the traumatised parts of yourself.

18 | The Serenity Prayer

God grant me the serenity to accept the things I cannot change;
Courage to change the things I can; And wisdom to know the
difference.

Amen.

Declare and Be Healed

- I let go of old attachments that have kept me bound to my painful past.
- I set my heart free from all the anger and bitterness of the past; I forgive all that I have to forgive.
- I choose to practice nonattachment, accepting what comes and allowing it to leave when it is time.
- I take full responsibility and ownership for my own happiness, and I am fully responsible for making and keeping me happy.
- I forgive myself for past regrets, mistakes, and shortsightedness, which have made me act irresponsibly.
- I forgive myself for all the choices and decisions that were a result of lacking wisdom and insight.
- I choose to focus on the lessons of my painful experiences rather than the pain itself.
- I acknowledge that I am not what happened to me, but I can learn from what happened to me.

- I allow myself to fully feel my emotions while maintaining awareness that I am not the emotion.
- I am healed, whole and complete.
- I appreciate the present moment. Daily, I practice being present and being one with the present moment.
- I increase awareness of my thoughts and how they contribute to my self-inflicted suffering.
- I change how I perceive and relate to suffering. I choose to see suffering as an unavoidable part of existence as opposed to something that must always be resisted.
- I choose to see pain and suffering as my teachers in this classroom of life.
- I affirm that both the light and the dark work together for my own good.
- I embrace every breath I take. I appreciate all the experiences that have shaped me, whether good or bad.
- I love, honour and appreciate every part of myself.

Conclusion

In the words of the enlightened, I shall conclude this piece. Iyanla Vanzant states, "The only thing you can do with a broken heart is to fix the mind". In concord with this statement, "In the book of Jeremiah, the Bible speaks of the human heart being sick or desperately wicked beyond cure. There is no cure for what is already beyond cure, except to fix the mind, to which the heart is a servant. The lack of insight into human behaviour has left many wounded and scared. But through this humble contribution to humanity, I hope that mankind will be enlightened and healed. Not all healing requires a medical prescription and concoctions, but even revelations and insights have the power to heal us.

I am fully persuaded in my spirit that this is the era of taking charge of our emotional healing and spiritual wholeness, and through this book, that era is being ushered to humanity. An awakening to truths and insights about the self is imperative and very much needed at this time. Many are suffering, but the real and actual cause is hidden from their eyes; they look and look but cannot see - they listen and listen but cannot hear it. Noticing suffering is easy, but seeing how one is contributing to it is what is difficult. The very same mind that can cause suffering when wrongly conditioned can bring healing to the heart and soul when properly conditioned. Allow yourself to unlearn and relearn; with the renewal of the mind comes the refreshing of the soul.

By becoming aware of the role our attachment plays in human suffering, we shall be in a better position to deal with it. Through certain religious and cultural conditionings, we lost touch with the very core and essence of our humanness, which resulted in us responding in detrimental ways to our human experiences. Our human experiences are real in all the forms they come in, whether traumatic or pleasurable, and they need to be given the honour and acknowledgement they deserve.

We all carry wounds and scars that do not show in the body yet deep inside, we know very well how much they have shaped who we are. Beyond the veil of separation and animosity lies something very beautiful and precious: the shared human experience that ties us together as children of this beautiful universe. What you will hear here is going to transform how you see. Like Jesus Christ, after having read the scroll in the synagogue, I also quote this proverb to you,

"PHYSICIAN, HEAL YOURSELF". This world that was framed through words will, in like manner, be healed through words.

www.ingramcontent.com/pod-product-compliance
Lightning Source LLC
LaVergne TN
LVHW051223200726

843510LV00011B/1465